AF295305

CBSE Term II
2022

Physical Education

Class XII

- Complete Theory in sync with Syllabus
- Case Based Questions
- Short/Long Answer Type Questions
- 3 Practice Papers with Explanation

Author
Reena Kar

arihant
ARIHANT PRAKASHAN (School Division Series)

ARIHANT PRAKASHAN (School Division Series)

© **Publisher**

No part of this publication may be re-produced, stored in a retrieval system or by any means, electronic, mechanical, photocopying, recording, scanning, web or otherwise without the written permission of the publisher. Arihant has obtained all the information in this book from the sources believed to be reliable and true. However, Arihant or its editors or authors or illustrators don't take any responsibility for the absolute accuracy of any information published and the damage or loss suffered thereupon.

All disputes subject to Meerut (UP) jurisdiction only.

卐 **Administrative & Production Offices**

Regd. Office

'Ramchhaya' 4577/15, Agarwal Road, Darya Ganj, New Delhi -110002
Tele: 011- 47630600, 43518550

卐 **Head Office**

Kalindi, TP Nagar, Meerut (UP) - 250002, Tel: 0121-7156203, 7156204

卐 **Sales & Support Offices**

Agra, Ahmedabad, Bengaluru, Bareilly, Chennai, Delhi, Guwahati, Hyderabad, Jaipur, Jhansi, Kolkata, Lucknow, Nagpur & Pune.

卐 **ISBN :** 978-93-25797-02-4

卐 **PRICE :** ₹125.00

PO No : TXT-XX-XXXXXXX-X-XX

Published by Arihant Publications (India) Ltd.

For further information about the books published by Arihant, log on to www.arihantbooks.com or e-mail at info@arihantbooks.com

Follow us on   

Contents

Watch Free Learning Videos

Subscribe **arihant** You Tube Channel

☑ Video Solutions of CBSE Sample Papers
☑ Chapterwise Important MCQs
☑ CBSE Updates

Syllabus CBSE Term II Class XII

*Unit No.	Name
3	**Yoga & Lifestyle**

Yoga & Lifestyle

- Asanas as preventive measures
- Obesity: Procedure, Benefits & contraindications for Vajrasana, Hastasana, Trikonasana, Ardh Matsyendrasana
- Diabetes: Procedure, Benefits & contraindications for Bhujangasana, Paschimottasana, Pavan Muktasana, Ardh Matsyendrasana
- Asthma: Procedure, Benefits & contraindications for Sukhasana, Chakrasana, Gomukhasana, Parvatasana, Bhujangasana, Paschimottasana, Matsyasana
- Hypertension: Tadasana, Vajrasana, Pavan Muktasana, Ardha Chakrasana, Bhujangasana, Sharasana

4　Physical Education & Sports for CWSN
(Children with Special Needs - DIVYANG)

- Concept of Disability & Disorder
- Types of Disability, its causes & nature (cognitive disability, intellectual disability, physical disability)
- Types of Disorder, its cause & nature (ADHD, SPD, ASD, ODD, OCD)
- Disability Etiquettes
- Strategies to make Physical Activities assessable for children with special need.

7　Physiology & Injuries in Sports

- Physiological factor determining component of Physical Fitness
- Effect of exercise on Cardio Respiratory System
- Effect of exercise on Muscular System
- Sports injuries: Classification (Soft Tissue Injuries:(Abrasion, Contusion, Laceration, Incision, Sprain & Strain) Bone & Joint Injuries: (Dislocation, Fractures: Stress Fracture, Green Stick, Communated, Transverse Oblique & Impacted) Causes, Prevention& treatment
- First Aid – Aims & Objectives

9　Physiology & Sports

- Personality; its definition & types – Trait & Types (Sheldon & Jung Classification) & Big Five Theory
- Motivation, its type & techniques
- Meaning, Concept & Types of Aggressions in Sports

10　Training in Sports

- Strength – Definition, types & methods of improving Strength – Isometric, Isotonic & Isokinetic
- Endurance - Definition, types & methods to develop Endurance – Continuous Training, Interval Training & Fartlek Training
- Speed – Definition, types & methods to develop Speed – Acceleration Run & Pace Run
- Flexibility – Definition, types & methods to improve flexibility
- Coordinative Abilities – Definition & types

CBSE Circular

Exam Scheme Term I & II

केन्द्रीय माध्यमिक शिक्षा बोर्ड

(शिक्षा मंत्रालय, भारत सरकार के अधीन एक स्वायत संगठन)

CENTRAL BOARD OF SECONDARY EDUCATION

(An Autonomous Organisation under the Ministryof Education, Govt. of India)

CBSE/DIR (ACAD)/2021

Date: July 05, 2021

Circular No: Acad-51/2021

All the Heads of Schools affiliated to CBSE

Subject: Special Scheme of Assessment for Board Examination Classes X and XII for the Session 2021-22

COVID 19 pandemic caused almost all CBSE schools to function in a virtual mode for most part of the academic session of 2020-21. Due to the extreme risk associated with the conduct of Board examinations during the second wave in April 2021, CBSE had to cancel both its class X and XII Board examinations of the year 2021 and results are to be declared on the basis of a credible, reliable, flexible and valid alternative assessment policy. This, in turn, also necessitated deliberations over alternative ways to look at the learning objectives as well as the conduct of the Board Examinations for the academic session 2021-22 in case the situation remains unfeasible.

CBSE has also held stake holder consultations with Government schools as well as private independent schools from across the country especially schools from the remote rural areas and a majority of them have requested for the rationalization of the syllabus, similar to last year in view of reduced time permitted for organizing online classes. The Board has also considered the concerns regarding differential availability of electronic gadgets, connectivity and effectiveness of online teaching and other socio-economic issues specially with respect to students from economically weaker section and those residing in far flung areas of the country. In a survey conducted by CBSE, it was revealed that the rationalized syllabus notified for the session 2020-21 was effective for schools in covering the syllabus and helped learners in achieving learning objectives in a less stressful manner.

In the above backdrop and in line with the Board's continued focus on assessing stipulated learning outcomes by making the examinations competencies and core concepts based, student-centric, transparent, technology-driven, and having advance provision of alternatives for different future scenarios, the following schemes are introduced for the Academic Session for Class X and Class XII 2021-22.

केन्द्रीय माध्यमिक शिक्षा बोर्ड

(शिक्षा मंत्रालय, भारत सरकार के अधीन एक स्वायत संगठन)

CENTRAL BOARD OF SECONDARY EDUCATION

(An Autonomous Organisation under the Ministryof Education, Govt. of India)

Special Scheme for 2021-22

A. Academic session to be divided into 2 Terms with approximately 50% syllabus in each term:

The syllabus for the Academic session 2021-22 will be divided into 2 terms by following a systematic approach by looking into the interconnectivity of concepts and topics by the Subject Experts and the Board will conduct examinations at the end of each term on the basis of the bifurcated syllabus. This is done to increase the probability of having a Board conducted classes X and XII examinations at the end of the academic session.

B. The syllabus for the Board examination 2021-22 will be rationalized similar to that of the last academic session to be notified in July 2021. For academic transactions, however, schools will follow the curriculum and syllabus released by the Board vide Circular no. F.1001/CBSE-Acad/Curriculum/2021 dated 31 March 2021. Schools will also use alternative academic calendar and inputs from the NCERT on transacting the curriculum.

C. Efforts will be made to make Internal Assessment/ Practical/ Project work more credible and valid as per the guidelines and Moderation Policy to be announced by the Board to ensure fair distribution of marks.

Details of Curriculum Transaction

- Schools will continue teaching in distance mode till the authorities permit in-person mode of teaching in schools.
- **Classes IX-X: Internal Assessment** (throughout the year-irrespective of Term I and II) would include the *3 periodic tests, student enrichment, portfolio and practical work/ speaking listening activities/ project.*
- **Classes XI-XII: Internal Assessment** (throughout the year-irrespective of Term I and II) would include end of topic or unit tests/ exploratory activities/ practicals/ projects.
- Schools would create a student profile for all assessment undertaken over the year and retain the evidences in digital format.
- CBSE will facilitate schools to upload marks of Internal Assessment on the CBSE IT platform.
- Guidelines for Internal Assessment for all subjects will also be released along with the rationalized term wise divided syllabus for the session 2021-22.The Board would also provide additional resources like sample assessments, question banks, teacher training etc. for more reliable and valid internal assessments.

केन्द्रीय माध्यमिक शिक्षा बोर्ड
(शिक्षा मंत्रालय, भारत सरकार के अधीन एक स्वायत संगठन)

CENTRAL BOARD OF SECONDARY EDUCATION
(An Autonomous Organisation under the Ministryof Education, Govt. of India)

Term I Examinations:

- At the end of the first term, the Board will organize **Term I Examination** in a flexible schedule to be conducted between November-December 2021 with a window period of 4-8 weeks for schools situated in different parts of country and abroad. Dates for conduct of examinations will be notified subsequently.

- The Question Paper will have Multiple Choice Questions (MCQ) including case-based MCQs and MCQs on assertion-reasoning type. Duration of test will be **90 minutes** and it will cover only the rationalized syllabus of **Term I only** (i.e. approx. 50% of the entire syllabus).

- Question Papers will be sent by the CBSE to schools along with marking scheme.

- The exams will be conducted under the supervision of the External Center Superintendents and Observers appointed by CBSE.

- The responses of students will be captured on OMR sheets which, after scanning may be directly uploaded at CBSE portal or alternatively may be evaluated and marks obtained will be uploaded by the school on the very same day. The final direction in this regard will be conveyed to schools by the Examination Unit of the Board.

- Marks of the **Term I** Examination will contribute to the final overall score of students.

Term II Examination/ Year-end Examination:

- At the end of the second term, the Board would organize **Term II or Year-end Examination** based on the rationalized syllabus of Term II only (i.e. approximately 50% of the entire syllabus).

- This examination would be held around **March-April 2022** at the examination centres fixed by the Board.

- The paper will be of **2 hours duration** and have questions of different formats (case-based/ situation based, open ended- short answer/ long answer type).

- In case the situation is not conducive for normal descriptive examination **a 90 minute MCQ based exam** will be conducted at the end of the Term II also.

- Marks of the Term II Examination would contribute to the final overall score.

केन्द्रीय माध्यमिक शिक्षा बोर्ड

(शिक्षा मंत्रालय, भारत सरकार के अधीन एक स्वायत संगठन)

CENTRAL BOARD OF SECONDARY EDUCATION

(An Autonomous Organisation under the Ministryof Education, Govt. of India)

Assessment / Examination as per different situations

A. In case the situation of the pandemic improves and students are able to come to schools or centres for taking the exams.

Board would conduct Term I and Term II examinations at schools/centres and the theory marks will be distributed equally between the two exams.

B. In case the situation of the pandemic forces complete closure of schools during November-December 2021, but Term II exams are held at schools or centres.

Term I MCQ based examination would be done by students online/offline from home - in this case, the weightage of this exam for the final score would be reduced, and weightage of Term II exams will be increased for declaration of final result.

C. In case the situation of the pandemic forces complete closure of schools during March-April 2022, but Term I exams are held at schools or centres.

Results would be based on the performance of students on Term I MCQ based examination and internal assessments. The weightage of marks of Term I examination conducted by the Board will be increased to provide year end results of candidates.

D. In case the situation of the pandemic forces complete closure of schools and Board conducted Term I and II exams are taken by the candidates from home in the session 2021-22.

Results would be computed on the basis of the Internal Assessment/Practical/Project Work and Theory marks of Term-I and II exams taken by the candidate from home in Class X / XII subject to the moderation or other measures to ensure validity and reliability of the assessment.

In all the above cases, data analysis of marks of students will be undertaken to ensure the integrity of internal assessments and home based exams.

Dr. Joseph Emmanuel
Director (Academics)

CHAPTER 01

Yoga and Lifestyle

In this Chapter...

- Yoga
- Obesity
- Asthma
- Asanas as Preventive Measure
- Diabetes
- Hypertension

Yoga

The word 'yoga' is derived from Sanskrit word yuj which means 'to join'. **Patanjali** has described the word yuj as to 'stabilise the mind for the union of soul (*atma*) and God (*parmatma*)'.

It simply refers to the unity of body, mind and spirit. It is like uniting the individual self with the universal self. The power of yoga is in its simplicity, diversity, and flexibility.

Yoga teaches to balance the mental urge to push, control and be assertive with the impulse to yield, submit and be passive. There are eight elements of yoga. They are Yama, Niyama, Asana, Pranayama, Pratyahara, Dharana, Dhyana and Samadhi.

Asanas as Preventive Measure

Asanas can be defined as "an ability to put body in such position, that will make organs and glands of body more efficient, which subsequently improves health of mind and body."

Asanas are beneficial for the mind, psyche and chakras (energy centres), it also prevent people from many types of lifestyle diseases. It also helps in relieving stress, treating anxiety and make a person mentally rejuvenated.

These are of different types *viz.* **meditative**, **relaxative** and **corrective** asanas.

Importance of Asanas

The importance of Asanas are as follows

- Asanas play a significant role in making our muscles strong.
- Asanas improves flexibility of body. It enhances functioning of bones, **cartilages**[1] and ligament.
- Asanas ensure smooth functioning of the organ systems in our body such as digestive system, cardiovascular system and circulatory system.
- Performing asanas regularly helps in curing many diseases and maintains good health, which increases longevity.

Doing many asanas help in preventing lifestyle diseases like obesity, diabetes, asthma and hypertension. These are discussed as follows

Obesity

Obesity is referred to a medical condition in which excess body fat is accumulated to the extent that it has a negative effect on health.

Generally, people are considered obese when their **Body Mass Index** (BMI) is more than 30.

Obesity leads to various diseases like diabetes, hypertension, cardiovascular diseases, osteoarthritis and depression. This is because due to the excess body fat, the organs inside the body are not able to function properly.

---

1 Cartilage is a non-vascular type of supporting tissue that is found throughout the body.

Causes

- Excess consumption of fats, sugar and calorie-rich foods.
- Improper functioning of certain glands such as endocrine gland system.
- Lack of exercises, less physical activities and sedentary lifestyle.

Symptoms

- Increase in weight constantly.
- Increase in laziness and rise in intake of food.
- Retardness in mental and emotional activities.
- Frustration and depression.

Preventions

- Take food which contain less fat, fibre-rich vegetables and fruits.
- Reduce the consumption of fats, sweets and junk foods.
- Stop addictions of smoking, drinking and other drugs.
- Increase physical activities, doing regular exercises.

Asanas for Obesity

Obesity can be prevented as well as cured by performing various asanas like *Vajrasana, Hastasana, Trikonasana* and *Ardha Matsyendrasana*.

These asanas are discussed in detail as follows

Vajrasana (Thunderbolt Pose)

Procedure

- It is done in sitting posture.
- Knee down on floor and sit on your heels. Rest your buttocks on the heels and the thighs on the calf muscles. Toe and knee should touch the floor.
- Keep the hands on the knees and keep the head straight.
- Concentrate on breathing, start inhalation and exhalation.

Benefits

- It ensures proper blood flow in the lower pelvic region and increases the efficiency of the digestive system.
- It helps to prevent acidity and ulcers by improving the digestion.
- It is a good meditative pose for those suffering from sciatica[2] and severe lower back problems.
- Supta Vajrasana strengthens the muscles in back, neck and chest regions.
- It reduces stress, blood pressure and improves blood circulation to lower abdominal region.
- The problems related to menstruation are cured by it.
- It enhances memory power by improving concentration.

- It also help in reducing hip fat and removes postural defects.

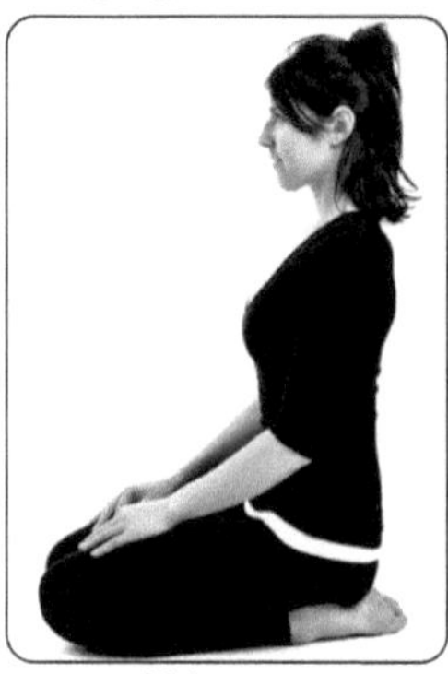
Vajrasana

Contraindications

- Vajrasana should not be practised by those suffering from severe knee pain and spinal column problem.
- This asana should be avoided by patients and who had recent surgery of legs or waist.
- If any pain is felt in the ankles during Vajrasana, then immediately release the pose and massage the ankle with the hands.

Hastasana

Hastasana is of two types *viz.* **Pada Hastasana** and **Urdhva Hastasana**. These are discussed below

Pada Hastasana

Procedure

- Stand straight and join the feet together, hand to the side of the body.
- Exhale and bend forward until the fingers or palms of the hands touches the floor, either side of the feet.
- Keep the knees straight and try to touch knees with the forehead and try to contract the abdomen.
- After few minutes, release the hand and slowly straighten the body keeping the neck down.

Pada Hastasana

---

2 Sciatica refers to pain that radiates along the path of sciatic nerve which branches from your lower back through your hips and buttocks and down each leg.

Benefits

- It reduces stress, anxiety, fatigue and helps to eliminate excess belly fat.
- It improves blood circulation.
- It increases concentration and speed up metabolism.
- It improves balance, posture and flexibility.

Contraindications

- A person who is suffering through spinal problem or having neck or knee problem should avoid doing it.
- Also avoid if you have any type of knee or neck injury.

Urdhva Hastasana

Procedure

- Stand straight and join the feet together, then, gently raise your hand upward without bending the shoulders, bring your arms together over your head.
- Expand the elbows completely and reach upwards. Then slightly slant your head backwards and look at the thumbs.
- Shoulder blades must be pressed firmly on your back.

Urdhva Hastasana

Benefits

- It stretches the complete body and provides a good massage to the arms, spine, upper and lower back, ankles, hands, shoulders, calf muscles and thighs.
- It enhances the functioning of digestive system and tightens the abdomen.
- This asana helps in improving the blood circulation of the body and enhances posture.
- It helps in easing sciatica.

Contraindications

- Avoid in case of shoulder or neck injuries.
- Avoid if experiencing dizziness while staring upwards and in case of any other medical concerns.

Trikonasana (Triangle Pose)

Procedure

- This is a standing posture.
- With an exhalation, step your feet 3-4 feet apart.
- Raise both the hands till they are in line with each other, parallel to the ground. Inhale when you are raising the hands.
- Now, bend towards the right and bend the trunk sideways and touch the right foot with the hands. Look up at the left hand.
- Return to the standing position.
- Repeat this with the left hand touching the left foot.

Benefits

- It strengthens the legs, knees, ankles, arms and chest.
- It stretches and opens the lower back region, groin area, hamstrings, calves, shoulders, chest, arms and spine.
- It enhances mental and physical equilibrium.
- It helps in improving digestion.
- It helps in reducing excess body weight and fat around the waist line.

Trikonasana

Contraindications

- Avoid doing this if suffering from migraine, diarrhoea, neck and back injuries.
- Those with high blood pressure may do this pose but without raising their hand overhead, as this may further raise the blood pressure.

Ardha Matsyendrasana
(Half Spinal Twist Pose)

Procedure

- This is done in sitting posture.
- Sit with legs straight and stretched in front of you.

- Bend the left leg and bring it close to the body. Place it under the right buttocks.
- Then, place the right leg next to the left knee by taking it over the knee.
- Twist your waist, neck and shoulders over your right shoulder. While doing it, keep your spine straight.
- Place the right hand behind and the left hand on the right knee.
- Then repeat the procedure with the other leg.

Benefits

- It is one of the best poses to improve the flexibility of the spine. It energises the spine.
- It stretches the shoulders, hips and neck.
- It stimulates the digestive enzymes in the belly which helps in reducing belly fat.
- It improves the working of kidneys, pancreas and small intestines.

Ardha Matsyendrasana

Contraindications

- Avoid during pregnancy and menstruation due to the strong twist in the abdomen.
- People with heart, abdominal or brain surgeries or having ulcer, slip disc should avoid this asana.

Diabetes

Diabetes is a disease in which the pancreas fail to produce insulin or is unable to use the insulin produced in an effective manner.

Insulin is a harmone produced by the pancreas that helps glucose, present in the blood, to enter the cells in our body and provide energy.

It is of two types *viz.* **Type I** and **Type II**. In Type I diabetes, the body is unable to produce insulin and in Type II diabetes, body produces insulin, but unable to use it effectively.

It can lead to **renal** (kidney) **failure, loss of vision, amputation of limbs** and **cardiovascular diseases**.

Causes

- Overweight, obesity and lack of physical activities.
- Genes and family history or hereditary factors.
- Gestational diabetes occur when the pancreas can't make enough insulin.
- Type I diabetes occurs when your immune system attacks and destroys the insulin.
- Type II diabetes is caused by several factors, including lifestyle factors and genes.

Symptoms

- Increase in thirst, hunger and fatigue.
- Frequent urination.
- Blurred vision.
- Numbness or tingling in feet and hands.

Preventions

- Eat whole grains like brown rice, oatmeal, millets, lightly cooked fresh vegetables, and fresh fruits.
- Avoid white bread, white rice, processed food, sugary drinks, jam, jelly, canned vegetables and fruits.
- Do regular exercises and other physical activities.

Asanas for Diabetes

Asanas like *Bhujangasana, Paschimottanasana, Pavanamuktasana* and *Ardha Matsyendrasana* can help in preventing and curing diabetes.

These asanas are discussed in detail as follows

Bhujangasana (The Cobra Pose)

Procedure

- This is done in lying posture.
- Lie on the stomach and rest forehead on the floor.
- Keep the feet and toes together and touch the ground.
- Place the hands at shoulder level and palms on floor.
- Inhale and lift the head, chest, abdomen up towards roof and keep the navel on the floor.
- Pull your torso back and off the floor with support of your hands.

Benefits

- It improves the blood circulation in body.
- It decreases menstrual irregularities in females.
- It strengthens muscles of chest, shoulders, arms and abdomen.
- It is effective in urine disorder.
- It improves the function of liver, kidney, pancreas, gall bladder and reproductive organs.
- It stretches the muscles of the chest, heart and lungs.

- It expands the ribcage and improves lung capacity.
- It enhances blood circulation, calms the nerves, relieves mental stress and reduces headache.

Bhujangasana

Contraindications

- Avoid during pregnancy.
- It should be avoided by persons who are suffering from ulcer, heart problem or any surgeries of spine.

Paschimottanasana

Procedure

- This is done in sitting posture.
- Sit on the floor with the legs stretched out.
- Bend forwards and hold the big toes with the middle and index fingers.
- Then, take five deep breaths and try to touch the knees with your forehead.

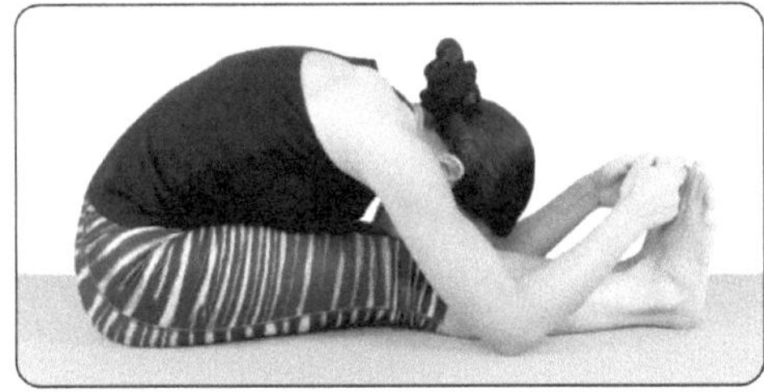
Paschimottanasana

Benefits

- It stretches hamstrings, spine, shoulders and hip joints.
- It enhances secretion of insulin from pancreas and improves digestion.
- It reduces **headache**, **anxiety**, **insomnia** and **sinusitis**[3].
- It reduces abdominal fats and increases metabolism.
- It relieves stress, anger and irritability.
- It massages and tones the shoulders, chest and spine muscles.

Contraindications

- Pregnant women should avoid this asana.

- It should be avoided by person suffering from respiratory and spinal problem.
- Ulcer patient should also avoid this asana.

Pavanamuktasana

Procedure

- This is done in lying position.
- Lie flat on the back and keep the legs straight.
- Inhale slowly and lift the legs and bend the knees. Bring upwards to the chest till the thigh touches the stomach.
- Hug the knees and lock the fingers.
- Place the nose tip between the knees.
- Exhale slowly and come back to the original position.

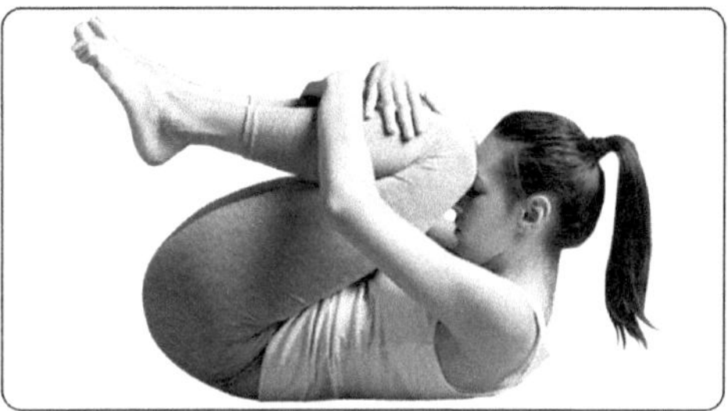
Pavanamuktasana

Benefits

- It cures acidity, indigestion and constipation.
- It is helpful for those suffering from gastrointestinal problems, arthritis, heart problems and waist and back pain.
- It is very beneficial for reproductive organs and for menstruation disorder.
- It strengthens muscles of back and abdomen.
- It helps in relieving stress.
- It cures digestive problems and lowers the risk of heart diseases.

Contraindications

- Those who are suffering from **high blood pressure**, **hernia**, **heart problems** and **ulcer** should avoid.

Note : For **Ardha Matsyendrasana's** Procedure, Benefits and Contraindications refer to Page 3 and 4.

Asthma

Asthma is a condition in which a person's airways in the lungs become narrow. Due to narrowness, air flow is obstructed. It creates breathing problem in a person.

It is a long-term inflammatory disease. In this disease, the airways also swell up and produce extra mucus, which enhances breathing problem.

---

3 Sinusitis It is an inflammation of the sinuses that can cause them to get blocked and filled with fluid.

The coughing usually occurs at night or early in the morning. It is more complex from other diseases, as it cannot be cured or treated but its symptoms can be controlled.

Causes

- Allergy from airborne substances like pollen grains, dust mites, molds, spores etc.
- Air pollutants and irritants like smoke suspended in the air.
- Respiratory infections like common cold.
- It can also occur due to genetic factors.

Symptoms

- Shortness of breath
- Coughing/sneezing too much
- Frequent respiratory infections
- Chest tightness
- Wheezing

Preventions

- Keep the room, bed, pillows dust free.
- Avoid asthma-triggers like pollens, mole, cold air to prevent asthma attacks.
- Follow prescribed medication.

Asanas for Asthma

Asanas which can cure or help in managing asthma includes *Sukhasana, Chakrasana, Gomukhasana, Parvatasana, Bhujangasana, Paschimottanasana* and *Matsyasana*.

These asanas are discussed in detail below

Sukhasana

Procedure

- This is done in sitting position.
- Sit cross legged on the floor or any other flat surface.
- Bend your knees, and cross your right shin in front of your left shin.
- Move the knees closer until your feet is directly underneath them.
- Place both the palms on your knees, close your eyes and breathe slowly.
- Continue breathing in the same way for 5 minutes.

Benefits

- It helps to make the back stronger and elongate the muscles of knees, ankles and spine.
- It is beneficial for opening the muscles of groin, hips and the outer thighs.

- It relieves from physical and mental tiredness and removes stress.

Sukhasana

Contraindications

- In case of severe knee and back injury, it is required to sit over the folded blanket or take the assistance of bolster or pillow.
- Person suffering from slipped disc problem should avoid it.

Chakrasana (Wheel Pose)

Procedure

- This is done in lying posture.
- Lie down properly and look upward.
- Bring the feet closer to the hips and bend knees upward; keep a distance of about one foot between the feet.
- Bring your palms under your shoulder.
- Gradually lift up the body in air by balancing on palms and feet and rotate the head backward along with hands slowly.
- Reach the final position by stretching the whole body to form a position of a semi-circle.
- To go back to original position, slowly lower down the body and release the hands and feet.

Chakrasana

Benefits

- It is good for infertility and osteoporosis.
- It strengthens **arms**, **shoulders**, **hands**, **wrists**, **legs**, **buttocks**, **abdomen** and **spine**.
- It stretches the chest and lungs which is good for treating asthma.
- It helps to stimulate the thyroid and pituitary glands.
- It reduces anxiety, stress and mental fatigue.

Contraindications

- Those who are suffering from diarrhoea, heart problems, hernia hypertension, ankle and spine pain should avoid it.
- Avoid during pregnancy.

Gomukhasana (Cow Face Pose)

Procedure

- This is done in sitting position.
- Sit straight and stretch both legs together in front.
- Fold right leg at the knee and place it on the ground by the side of the left buttock.
- Bringing the left leg from above the right leg, place it on the ground by the side of the right buttock.
- Fold your left arm and place it behind your back. Then, take your right hand over your right shoulder, and stretch it as much as you can until it reaches your left hand.
- Repeat it with other leg.

Benefits

- It helps in stretching and strengthen the muscles of the ankles, hips and thighs, shoulders, triceps, inner armpits and chest.
- It is helpful in curing of sciatica, reduces stress and anxiety.
- It improves the functioning of lungs.

Gomukhasana

Contraindications

- Those who are suffering from shoulder, knee or back pain should avoid it.
- Pregnant women should avoid it.

Parvatasana (Mountain Pose)

Procedure

- Sit down on the floor in cross-legged position.
- Bring the hands in the front and interlock the fingers.
- Breathe out and stretch the hands over the head. Keep the fingers interlocked.
- Pull the torso in upward direction and stretch for a few minutes.
- Hold in this position for sometime and then return to normal position.

Parvatasana

Benefits

- It helps in improving the blood circulation.
- It helps in curing respiratory disorders that causes asthma.
- It reduces mental fatigue and improves memory.
- It reduces muscle pain, especially in back and neck regions.

Contraindications

- Don't bend the elbow or overstrain the knees and avoid hunching of the back during sitting position.

Note : For ***Bhujangasana's*** *Procedure, Benefits and Contraindications refer to Page 4 and for* ***Paschimottanasana's*** *Procedure, Benefits and Contraindications refer to Page 5.*

Matsyasana (Fish Pose)

Procedure

- This asana is done in lying pose.
- Lift your hips and tuck your hands slightly beneath your buttocks, palms facing down. Kness can either be bent or extended. Draw your forearms and elbows in towards your body.

- With inhale, bend your elbows and press firmly on your forearms and elbows to lift your head and upper body away from the floor.
- Firm your shoulder blades into your back and lift your chest higher towards the ceiling, elongate your spine.
- Bring the crown of your head down on the floor.
- Remain in this position for a few minutes.

Matsyasana

Benefits

- It stretches the neck muscles and shoulders and prevents stiffness.
- This pose provides relief from respiratory disorders by encouraging deep breathing, as this pose increases lung capacity to a great extent.
- There is an increased supply of blood to the cervical and thoracic regions of the back that helps tone the **parathyroid**, **pituitary** and **pineal glands**.

Contraindications

- Individuals suffering from high or low blood pressure should avoid this posture.
- Women who are pregnant should not attempt this yoga pose.
- Injury in neck or any part of the lower back or middle back can make it difficult to practice this fish pose and hence should be avoided.

Hypertension

Hypertension is also known as **high blood pressure**. In hypertension, the blood pressure of body goes beyond 140/90 mm/Hg. The normal body pressure of an adult person is considered as 120/80 mm/Hg.

The situation of hypertension arises when heart pumps more blood than normal situation and arteries become narrower.

Earlier, it was considered as a middle-age problem but now-a-days, youngsters also suffer from this problem due to their faulty lifestyle.

Hypertension is a primary risk factor for cardiovascular disease, including stroke, heart attack and heart failure.

Causes

- Sedentary lifestyle (little or no physical activity) is one of most important reasons behind hypertension.

- Consumption of fatty foods, salt rich diets, alcohol and tobacco.
- Kidney diseases may also increase hypertension.

Symptoms

- Severe headaches.
- Nose bleeds frequently.
- Shortness of breath and severe anxiety.
- Spells of frequent anger and irritation.

Preventions

- Avoid canned foods, fatty foods, processed foods and reduce the salt intake to just 2,300 milligrams per day.
- Eat more fruits, vegetables, nuts, legumes, lean meat and poultry.
- Increase physical activities and reduce weight.

Asanas of Hypertension

To prevent and cure hypertension, perform various asanas that reduce stress and rejuvenate mind and body such as *Tadasana, Vajrasana, Pavanamuktasana, Ardha Chakrasana, Bhujangasana* and *Shavasana*.

These asanas are discussed in detail as follows

Tadasana (Mountain Pose)
Procedure

- This is done in standing position.
- Stand straight and join the feet together.
- Toes must touch each other and heels may be slightly apart.
- With deep inhalation, raise up both the arms and then interlock the fingers.
- Stretch your shoulders and chest upward.
- Hold for 4 to 8 breaths.
- Exhale and drop the shoulders down.

Tadasana

Benefits

- Knees, thighs and ankles become stronger.
- Buttocks and abdomen get toned.
- It also makes spine more agile.
- It helps in increasing height and improves balance.
- It regulates digestive, nervous and respiratory systems.

Contraindications

- Avoid during headaches or insomnia.
- Avoid during low blood pressure.

*Note : For **Vajrasana's** Procedure, Benefits and Contraindications refer to Page 2 and for **Pavanamuktasana's** Procedure, Benefits and Contraindications refer to Page 5.*

Ardha Chakrasana (Half Wheel Pose)

Procedure

- This is a standing pose.
- Stand straight and arms alongside the body.
- Balance the weight equally on both feet.
- Breath in, extend the arms overhead, palms facing each other.
- Bend backwards, push the pelvis forwards, keeping the arms in line with the ears, elbows and knees straight, head up and lift the chest up towards the ceiling.
- Breathing out, bring the arms down and relax.

Benefits

Ardha Chakrasana

- It stretches the front part of upper torso.
- It tones the arms and shoulder muscles.

- It helps in relieving constipation.
- It enhances flexibility of hip joints.
- It controls high blood pressure.
- It improves digestion and menstrual disorder.
- It also relieves stress and tension.

Contraindications

- It should be avoided by people who are having serious hip and spinal problems, high blood pressure, and brain ailments.
- Individuals suffering from peptic or duodenal ulcers and hernia should avoid it.
- Pregnant women should avoid it.

*Note : For **Bhujangasana's** Procedure, Benefits and Contraindications refer to Page 4.*

Shavasana (Corpse Pose)

Procedure

- This is done in lying position.
- Lie flat on the back, like in sleeping pose.
- Keep the arms at side and palms facing up and relax.
- Close the eyes and breathe deeply and slowly through the nostrils. Stay in this pose for 10 to 15 minutes.

Benefits

- It relaxes the whole body.
- It releases stress, fatigue, depression and tension.
- It improves concentration and cures insomnia.
- It helps to calm the mind and improves mental health.
- It regulates blood circulation.
- It gives new vigour to both mind and body simultaneously.

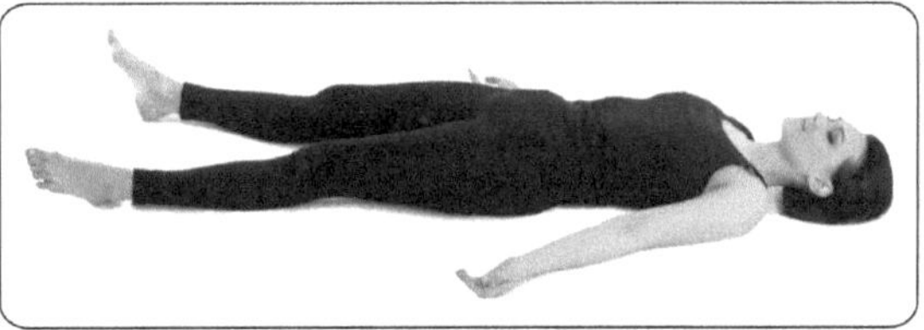

Shavasana

Contraindication

Usually, there is no contraindication of this asana, except where the doctor has advised not to lie on back.

Chapter Practice

PART 1

Objective Questions

• Multiple Choice Questions (MCQs)

1. The symptoms of obesity includes
   (a) Gaining weight
   (b) Retardness
   (c) Laziness
   (d) All of these

Ans. (d) The symptoms of obesity includes gaining weights which leads to laziness and retardness.

2. People are considered to suffer from obesity when their BMI is
   (a) less than 25
   (b) more than 25
   (c) more than 30
   (d) more than 35

Ans. (d) People are considered to suffer from obesity when their BMI is more than 35.

3. Which one of the following asanas is not a remedial asana for treating obesity?   **(CBSE 2020)**
   (a) Vajrasana
   (b) Tadasana
   (c) Trikonasana
   (d) Ardha Matsyendrasana

Ans. (b) Tadasana is a remedial asana for treating hypertension and not obesity. This asana relieves the mind from stress and makes a person more agile. It regulates our digestive system.

4. Which one of the following asanas can be performed immediately after the meals?   **(CBSE 2020)**
   (a) Chakrasana
   (b) Dhanurasana
   (c) Sukhasana
   (d) Vajrasana

Ans. (d) Vajrasana which is also called thunderbolt pose, increases the efficiency of the digestive system. Therefore it can be performed immediately after the meals.

5. Which lifestyle disease can be cured by practising the asana shown below.

   (a) Asthma
   (b) Hypertension
   (c) Obesity
   (d) All of these

Ans. (c) The asana shown in the image is Ardha-Matsyendrasana. Obesity can be cured by practising this asana.

6. Which hormone is related with the problem of diabetes?
   (a) Insulin
   (b) Calcitonin
   (c) Oxytocin
   (d) Estrogens

Ans. (a) The hormone called insulin is related with the problem of diabetes. This hormone is produced by the pancreas. Insufficient production of insulin or no production at all causes diabetes.

7. Ramya's mother was suffering from Type-II diabetes. Her doctor prescribed her some medicines and asked her to eat whole grains, avoid processed foods and do regular exercises to control the blood sugar levels.

   Blood sugar levels are controlled by ________ hormone.
   (a) Thyroxin
   (b) Progesterone
   (c) Insulin
   (d) Estrogen

Ans. (c) Blood sugar levels are controlled by Insulin hormone which is produced by the pancreas.

8. Shruti, a yoga instructor at XYZ school conducted a survey on which is the favourite asana of students. She was able to make a pie chart on the basis of the data.

On the basis of the chart answer the following question.

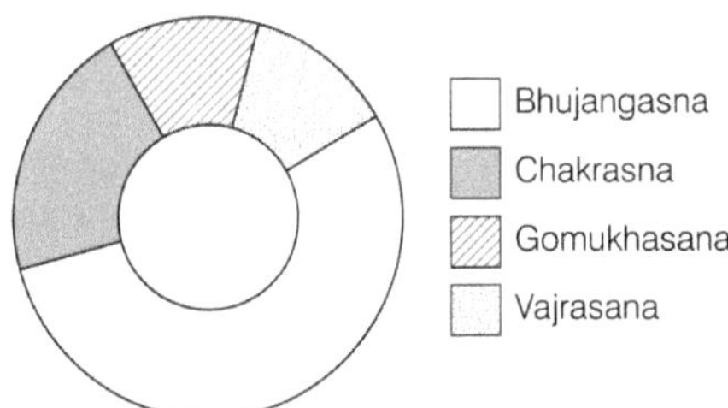

Which is the most famous asana?

(a) Bhujangasana (b) Chakrasana

(c) Gomukhasana (d) Vajrasana

Ans. (a) On the basis of pie chart, the most famous asana is Bhujangasana as large number of students like it.

9. Identify the asana shown below.

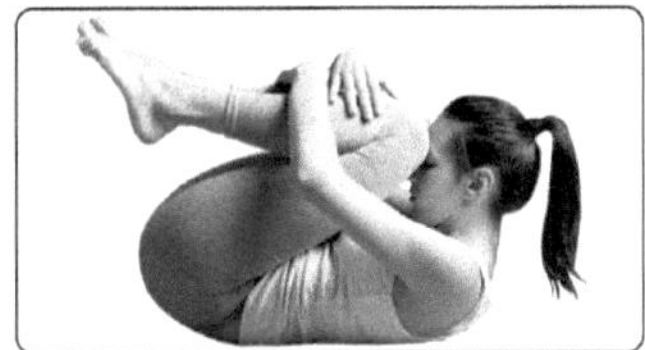

(a) Ardha Matseyendrasana (b) Bhujangasana

(c) Paschimottanasana (d) Pavanamuktasana

Ans. (d) The asana shown is pavanamuktasana. This asana is beneficial in curing diabetes. It also cures acidity, indigestion and constipation. It is done in lying position.

10. Ramya's mother was suffering from leg and back pain. She has undergone many treatments, but still, she is suffering from the problem. At last, she decided to meet a yoga instructor and discussed her problem. He prescribed some asanas.

Which of the following is suitable for Ramya mother's problem?

(a) Urdhva Hastasana (b) Pada Hastasana

(c) Tadasana (d) Gomukhasana

11. Mr. Mohan, aged 50 years is a bank employee and spends a lot of time sitting at one place. He developed certain symptoms like frequent urge for urination, excessive weight gain, anxiety, etc. After a medical check up, his doctor said that he was suffering from hypertension.

Which assanas are recommended for curing hypertension?

(a) Vajrasana

(b) Ardha Chakrasana

(c) Tadasana

(d) All of the above

Ans. (d) The asana recommended for curing hypertension are Tadasana, Vajrasana, Pavanamuktasana, Ardha Chakrasana, Bhujangasana and Shavasana. These asanas reduce stress and rejuvenate mind and body.

12. Due to back pain, Ameebh is suffering from round shoulders for which he is advised to _______ .

(a) hold the horizontal bar for sometime

(b) hold the vertical bar for sometime

(c) perform Pawanmuktasana

(d) All of the above

Ans. (a) Ameebh is advised to hold the horizontal bar for sometime.

13. Match the following.

	List I (Disease)		List II (Asana)
A.	Obesity	1.	Pavanamuktasana
B.	Diabetes	2.	Tadasana
C.	Asthma	3.	Hastasana
D.	Hypertension	4.	Chakrasana

Codes

	A	B	C	D
(a)	3	1	4	2
(b)	1	4	2	3
(c)	2	4	1	3
(d)	4	1	3	2

Ans. (a) The correct match is A-3, B-1, C-4 and D-2.

14. Match the following.

	List I (Asana)		List II (Other Name)
A.	Vajrasana	1.	Cobra pose
B.	Trikonasana	2.	Triangle pose
C.	Bhujangasana	3.	Mountain pose
D.	Parvatasana	4.	Thunderbolt pose

Codes

	A	B	C	D
(a)	3	1	2	4
(b)	2	1	3	4
(c)	4	2	1	3
(d)	1	3	4	2

Ans. (c) The correct match is A-4, B-2, C-1 and D-3.

• Assertion-Reason MCQs

Direction (Q. Nos. 1-4) *Each of these questions contains two statements, Assertion (A) and Reason (R). Each of these questions also has four alternative choices, any one of which is the correct answer. You have to select one of the codes (a), (b), (c) and (d) given below.*

Codes

(a) Both A and R are true and R is the correct explanation of A
(b) Both A and R are true, but R is not the correct explanation of A
(c) A is true, but R is false
(d) A is false, but R is true

1. Assertion (A) Everyone should do yoga daily.

Reason (R) Yoga helps in avoiding various lifestyle disease such as diabetes, obesity and cardiovascular disease.

Ans. (a) The assertion that everyone should do yoga daily is true as yoga exercises both, the mind and body.

The reason is also true as by doing yoga daily various lifestyle disease can be prevented. Yogic asanas stretches the body, improves functioning of organs, relaxes the mind. Thus, both A and R are true and R is the correct explanation of A.

2. Assertion (A) Vajrasana is also called as mountain pose.

Reason (R) Vajrasana is always done in sitting position.

Ans. (d) The assertion is false as Vajrasana is called thunderbolt pose and Parvatasana is called mountain pose.

The reason is true as the procedure to do Vajrasana is by sitting on the floor or on the mat. Thus, A is false, but R is true.

3. Assertion (A) Yoga teaches the balance of body and mind.

Reason (R) Postural deformities can be prevented by the regular practice of yoga.

Ans. (b) Assertion is correct as yogic asanas are done to improve and increase the functioning of bodily systems. It also relaxes the mind.

Reason is true as regular practice of yoga can cure and even prevent postural deformities. But R do not explains A as both talk about two different things. Thus, Both A and R are true, but R is not the correct explanation of A.

4. Assertion (A) Lifestyle diseases are very common now-a-days.

Reason (R) Improper eating and sedantary lifestyle leads to improper functioning of certain glands giving rise to such diseases.

Ans. (a) Assertion is true as there are some diseases which are on the rise like Diabetes, Hypertension, Asthma. These are called lifestyle diseases.

Reason is also true as the causes of these diseases are improper eating and sedentary lifestyle. The reason explains the assertion. Thus, both A and R are true and R is the correct explanation of A.

• Case Based MCQs

1. Neeti along with her father was regular at District Park in early morning. She realised that most of the children are obese. She along with her few classmates wanted to help those children. She discussed with her physical education teacher and the principal of the school. School decided to organise awareness rally for the neighbourhood.

(i) Obesity causes
   (a) underweight   (b) diabetes
   (c) hypertension   (d) Both (b) and (c)

Ans. (d) Obesity causes diabetes and hypertension.

(ii) Which of the following Asana (posture) is not used for curing obesity?
   (a) Ardha Matsyendrasana   (b) Vajrasana
   (c) Parvatasana   (d) Trikonasana

Ans. (c) Parvatasana is not used for curing obesity.

(iii) Choose the asana which is used for curing obesity.
   (a) Sukhasana   (b) Shavasana
   (c) Vajrasana   (d) Shalabhasana

Ans. (c) Vajrasana is used for curing obesity.

2. Geetha, the yoga teacher does regular yoga activities in her house with family. It helps to improve her family health. One day her neighbour, Sheela came to her house with her daughter. Sheela's daughter is 14-year old, but has short height. Geetha advised her to do some asanas regularly to increase her height.   **(CBSE Question Bank 2021)**

(i) Which asana can be advised by Geetha?
   (a) Tadasana   (b) Bhujangasana
   (c) Sukhasana   (d) Both (a) and (b)

Ans. (a) Tadasana can be advised by Geetha.

(ii) Vajrasana helps to relieve from
   (a) Back pain   (b) Constipation
   (c) Headache   (d) Both (a) and (b)

Ans. (d) Vajrasana helps to relieve from constipation and headache.

(iii) Which asana can be used to cure obesity?
   (a) Pavanamuktasana   (b) Matsyasana
   (c) Shavasana   (d) Trikonasana

Ans. (d) Trikonasana can be used to cure obesity.

PART 2

Subjective Questions

• Short Answer (SA) Type Questions

1. Explain the Yoga and Asana.

Ans. Yoga is derived from the Sanskrit word 'yuj'. It means the unity of body, mind and spirit. Patanjali has described 'Yoga' as a way to stable the mind for the union of soul (*atma*) and God (*parmatma*).

Asana refers to the position in which a person sits/stands to do yoga. Asanas are beneficial for the muscles, joints, cardiovascular system, nervous system and lymphatic system. It prevents body from various lifestyle diseases.

2. What are the benefits of doing various asanas?

Ans. The benefits of doing various asanas are as follows
- Asanas play a significant role in making our muscles strong.
- Asanas improve flexibility of body thus preventing injuries.
- Asanas ensure smooth functioning of the organs.
- Asanas help in mental development.
- Asanas help in relieving tension and stress.
- Asanas help in curing lifestyle diseases like diabetes and hypertension.

3. What is the role of yoga in preventing lifestyle diseases? **(CBSE 2019)**

Ans. Yoga plays prominent role in preventing lifestyle diseases are as follows
- Yoga gives relief from physical and mental ailments.
- Regular practice of yoga relieves mental stress. Yoga makes a person free from anger, anxiety and emotional disturbances.
- Cold, cough, insomnia, asthma, constipation, arthritis, acidity, diarrhoea etc. can be prevented with the regular practice of yogic asanas.
- Postural deformities can be prevented by the regular practice of yoga.

4. What is obesity? Is it a disease? Explain your answer.

Ans. Obesity is referred to medical condition in which excess body fat is accumulated to the extent that it has a negative effect on health.

Obesity in itself is not a disease but the condition of obesity leads to many diseases. This is because a person becomes extremely fat and the organs, glands, organ systems cannot function properly.

When the body does not function properly, then it gives birth to many diseases like diabetes, hypertension, cardiovascular diseases, etc.

5. Write the detail about the benefits of Urdhva Hastasana.

Ans. Benefits of Urdhva Hastasana are as follows
- It stretches the complete body and provides a good massage to the arms, spine, upper and lower back, ankles, hands, shoulders, calf muscles and thighs.
- It enhances the functioning of digestive system and increases the capacity of the lungs.
- This asana helps in improving the blood circulation of the body.
- It helps in improving the body postures.

6. Write down procedure of Trikonasana.

Ans. The procedure of Trikonasana is as follows
- Stand straight and hands along side.
- Raise both the hands till they are not in line with each other, parallel to the ground. Inhale when you are raising the hands.
- Now, bend towards the right and bend the trunk side ways and touch the right foot with the hands. Look up at the left hand.
- Return to the standing position.
- Repeat this with the left hand touching the left foot.

7. What are the ways to prevent diabetes.

Ans. The ways to prevent diabetes are as follows
- Reduce the consumption of white bread, rice, processed food, sugary drinks, jam, jelly etc.
- Eat whole grains like brown rice, oatmeal, millets, vegetables and fruits.
- Do physical exercises that include asanas like Bhujangasana, Paschimottasana, Pavanamuktasana and Ardha Matsyendrasana.

8. Explain the procedure of any one asana used to cure diabetes. **(CBSE 2020)**

Ans. Pavanamuktasana help in curing diabetes. Procedure of Pavanamuktasana is as follows
- This is done in lying position.
- Lie flat on the back, keep the legs straight and relax your body.
- Inhale slowly and lift the legs and bend on the knees. Bring upwards to the chest till the thigh touches the stomach.
- Hug the knees and lock the fingers.
- Place the nose tip between the knees.
- Exhale slowly and come back to the original position.

9. Explain about the procedure of 'Bhujangasana'.
(**CBSE 2019**)

Ans. The procedure of Bhujangasana is as follows
- This is done in lying posture.
- Lie on the stomach and rest forehead on the floor.
- Keep the feet and toes together and touch the ground.
- Place the hands at shoulder level and palms on floor.
- Inhale and lift the head, chest, abdomen up towards roof and keep the navel on the floor.
- Pull your torso back and off the floor with support of your hands.

10. What are the advantages of Bhujangasana?

Ans. The advantages of Bhujangasana are as follows
- It improves the blood circulation in body.
- It decreases menstrual irregularities in females.
- It strengthens muscles of chest, shoulders, arms and abdomen.
- It is effective in urine disorder.
- It improves the functioning of reproductive organ.
- It improves the function of liver, kidney, pancreas and gall bladder.

11. Explain the procedures of Paschimottanasana.

Ans. The procedure of doing this asana is as follows
- This is done in sitting posture.
- Sit on the floor with the outstretched legs.
- Sit straight, raise both arms above your head and stretch up.
- Bend forwards and hold the big toes with the middle and index fingers.
- Then, exhale out slowly and try to touch the knees with your forehead.

12. Differentiate between Paschimottanasana and Pavanamuktasana.

Ans. Differentiate between Paschimottanasana and Pavanamuktasana are as follows

Paschimottanasana	Pavanamuktasana
This asana is done in sitting position.	This asana is done in lying position
It is beneficial for spine, shoulders and hip joints.	It is beneficial for internal organs like liver, kidney.
This asana is beneficial in curing Diabetes and Asthma.	This asana is beneficial for curing Diabetes and Hypertension.

13. What are main causes of asthma and what symptoms does it shows?

Ans. Main causes of asthma are as follows
- Allergy from airborne substances like pollen grains, dust mites, molds, spores etc.
- Air pollutants and irritants like smoke suspended in the air.
- Respiratory infections like common cold.
- It can also occur due to genetic factors.

Symptoms of asthma are as follows
- Shortness of breath.
- Coughing/sneezing too much.
- Frequent respiratory infections.
- Chest tightness.
- Wheezing.

14. What do you understand by hypertension? Describe the procedure for performing any one Yogic asana which reduces hypertension.

Ans. Hypertension occurs when the blood pressure of a person become abnormally high i.e. beyond the acceptable limits.

One Yogic asana which reduces hypertension is the Tadasana (Mountain Pose or Tree Pose). It is performed in the following ways
- Stand erect and place your legs slightly apart, with your hands hanging alongside your body.
- Make your thigh muscles firm. Then lift your kneecaps while ensuring you do not harden the lower part of your belly.
- Hold the pose for 10-20 seconds and return to normal position. Then repeat 10 times.

15. State the contraindications of Gomukhasana and benefits of Shavasana.

Ans. There are following contraindications of Gomukhasana
- Those who are suffering from shoulder, knee or back pain should avoid it.
- Pregnant women should avoid it.

There are following benefits of Shavasana
- It relaxes the whole body.
- It releases stress, fatigue, depression and tension.
- It improves concentration and cures insomnia.
- It helps to calm the mind and improves mental health.
- It regulates blood circulation.

• Long Answer (LA) Type Questions

1. Explain the contraindications of Pada Hastasana, Ardha Matsyendrasana and Urdhva Hastasana.

Ans. Contraindications of Pada Hastasana are as follows
- A person who is suffering through spinal problem should avoid doing it.
- Also avoid, if you have any type of knee or neck injury.

Contraindications of Ardha Matsyendrasana are as follows
- Avoid during pregnancy and menstruation due to the strong twist in the abdomen.
- People with heart, abdominal or brain surgeries should avoid this asana.
- Those who are having peptic ulcer or hernia should avoid it.
- Those with severe spinal problems should avoid it.
- Those with mild slipped disc can do it but in severe cases it should be avoided.

Contraindications of Urdhva Hastasana are
- Avoid in case of shoulder or neck injuries.
- Avoid, if experiencing dizziness while staring upwards and in case of any other medical concerns.

2. The modern lifestyle is the root cause of many diseases. Justify the statement.

Ans. It is true that modern lifestyle is the root cause of many diseases. This type of lifestyle promotes more of sedentary work.

In the absence of proper amount of physical activities, the body tends to gain weight that gives rise to obesity.

Obesity causes improper functioning of the organs and organ systems. It also increases lethargyness and reduces the rate of metabolism.

Consuming excess amount of fat and not burning enough calories causes various diseases like hypertension and diabetes. Air pollution and irritants like smoke, lead which are suspended in the air causes respiratory infections and asthma. The air pollution is also a result of modern lifestyle as it is caused by burning of fossil fuels.

Another result of modern lifestyle is the rise in eating of processed foods, canned foods, sugar drinks, that have high calories.

3. Which are the asanas Practiced for Preventing asthma? Give benefits and contradications of any two asanas.

Ans. Asana practiced for preventing asthama are

Sukhasana

Benefits
- It helps to make the back stronger and elongates the knees and ankles.

- It is beneficial for opening the muscles of the groin, hips and outer thighs.
- It relieves physical and mental tiredness and eliminates worries from the mind.

Contraindications
- In case of severe knee and back injury, it is required to sit over a folded blanket or take the assistance of a bolster or pillow.
- If difficulties are faced in this pose, then try placing the blanket or bolster under the thighs.

Chakrasana (Wheel Pose)

Benefits
- It helps to strengthen the liver, pancreas, kidneys and heart.
- It is good for infertility, asthma and osteoporosis.
- It strengthens the arms, shoulders, hands, wrists, legs, buttocks, abdomen and spine.
- It stretches the chest and lungs.

Contraindications
- These who are suffering from diarrhoea, heart problems and hernia should avoid this asana.
- Those who have wrist, ankles and spine pain should avoid it.
- Those with hypertension or hypotension should avoid this asana.

4. What are the procedures of Parvatasana and Ardha Chakrasana?

Ans. Procedure of Parvatasana is as follows
- Sit down on the floor in (cross- legged position).
- Bring the hands in the front and interlock the fingers.
- Breathe out and move the hands over the head. Keep the fingers interlocked and stretch hands upwards.
- Pull the torso in upward direction and stretch.
- Hold in this position for sometime and then return to normal position.

Procedure of Ardha Chakrasana is as follows
- This is a standing position.
- Stand straight and arms alongside the body.
- Balance the weight equally on both feet.
- Breath in, extend the arms overhead, palms facing each other.
- Bend backwards, push the pelvis forwards, keeping the arms in line with the ears, elbows and knees straight, head up, and lifting the chest upward.
- Breathing out, bring the arms down and relax.

5. Explain the procedure, benefits and contraindications of Tadasana. **(CBSE 2018)**

Ans. **Tadasana** (Mountain Pose)

Procedure of Tadasana is as follows

- This is done in standing position.
- Stand straight and join the feet together.
- Toes must touch each other and heels may be slightly apart.
- With deep inhalation, raise up both the arms and then interlock the fingers.
- Stretch your shoulders and chest upwards.
- Hold for 4 to 8 breaths.
- Exhale and drop the shoulders down.

Benefits of Tadasana are as follows

- It helps in correcting the body posture.
- It increases the flexibility of the ankles, thighs and joints.
- Buttocks and abdomen get toned.
- It helps in increasing height and improves balance.

Contraindications of Tadasana are as follows

- Avoid during headaches.
- Avoid during insomnia.
- Avoid during low blood pressure.

● Case Based Questions

1. Mehak, a Yoga instructor at XYZ School was consulted by a student of class XI in relation to her overweight. The child wants to do asanas to reduce her weight.

Based on this case answer the following question

(i) What might be the causes of Mehak over-weight?

Ans. The causes for Mehak's overweight are excess consumption of fats, sugar, calorie rich foods, lack of exercises and improper functioning of glands.

(ii) In which way Mehak can make out that the student is overweight or obese?

Ans. Mehak can make out the student's overweight by determining the Body Mass Index. If the BMI is more than 30 then the student is obese and if between 24.5 to 29.5 then overweight.

2. Mr. Anil aged 45 years is diagnosed with Diabetes. He is obese and has a sedentary lifestyle. He is having a family history of Diabetes.

Based on this case, answer the following questions.

(i) How many types of Diabetes are there?

Ans. There are two types of Diabetes. Type I in which insulin is not produced in the body and Type II in which body is unable to use it effectively.

(ii) Which asanas can be recommended for Mr. Anil?

Ans. To cure diabetes, Bhujangasana and Paschimottanasana can be recommended for Mr. Anil.

3. Asanas are defined as an ability to put body in a position that will make organs and glands of the body more efficient. This subsequently improves health of mind and body. Doing certain asanas regularly prevents and even cures many lifestyle diseases like hypertension, diabetes, asthma and reduces obesity. Based on this, answer the following questions.

(i) What is the importance of asanas?

Ans. Asanas improves flexibility of the body, enhances functioning of bones, muscles and ligaments.

(ii) How asanas rejuvenate the mind?

Ans. Asanas help in relieving stress, treating anxiety and make a person mentally rejuvenated.

Chapter Test

Multiple Choice Questions

1. The word Yoga is derived from
   (a) Yog
   (b) Yug
   (b) Yuj
   (d) Yoj

2. Obesity is result of which of the following factor?
   (a) Underweight
   (c) Diabetes
   (b) Excess fat in body
   (d) Back pain

3. Find the incorrect match.
   (a) Urdhva Hastasana - Obesity
   (c) Matsyasana - Diabetes
   (b) Gomukhasana - Asthma
   (d) Tadasana - Hypertension

4. In this lifestyle disease, the coughing usually occurs at night or early in the morning. It is more complex than other diseases, as it cannot be cured or treated but its symptoms can be controlled.

   Which lifestyle disease is being talked about in this passage?
   (a) Asthma
   (c) Hypertension
   (b) Cold
   (d) Flu

Short Answer Type Questions

5. Explain the benefits of Ardh-Matsyendrasana.
6. Write the steps to perform Vajrasana.
7. What are the contraindications of Ardh Matsyendrasana?
8. Explain the benefits of doing shavasana.
9. In what way Ardha Chakrasana is useful in giving a healthy lifestyle.

Long Answer Type Questions

10. Explain the causes, symptoms and prevention of Asthma.
11. "Practising Yoga-asanas regularly can prevent many diseases." Justify.

Answers

1. (b)   *2.* (b)   *3.* (d)   *4.* (a)

CHAPTER 02

Physical Education and Sports for CWSN
(Children With Special Needs : Divyang)

In this Chapter...

- Concept of Disability and Types
- Concept of Disorder and Types
- Disability Etiquettes
- Strategies to Make Physical Education Assessable

The phrase 'differently abled' was first proposed in 1980s as an alternative to terms like 'disabled', 'handicapped', etc. on the grounds that it gave a more positive message to the society and to avoid discrimination.

Disability and **disorder** are two separate terms that stand for different types of physical and mental conditions. Disability, whether it is physical or mental, is permanent in nature but a disorder can be temporary or permanent.

Concept of Disability

Disability is a **physical, mental, cognitive** or **developmental** condition that impairs, interferes with or limits a person's ability to engage in certain tasks or actions or participate in typical daily activities and interactions.

Disability may be present since birth or acquired during the liftime of the person. Disability reduces the functional ability of a person and limits the activities of that person.

Therefore, disability is conceptualised as multi-dimensional as it affects a person's life in many ways. It has been defined differently in different societies of the world.

According to **WHO**, "Disability is a restriction or lack of ability to perform an activity in the manner or within the range considered normal for a human being."

"A disability is defined as a condition or function judged to be significantly impaired relative to the usual standard of an individual or group."

Types of Disability

Disability is conceptualised as multi-dimensional as it may affect the organs and body parts of a person in many ways.

Disability is of many types like **cognitive disability, intellectual disability, physical disability**, etc.

These types of disabilities are discussed as follows

Cognitive Disability

Cognitive disability is a disability that impacts an individual's ability to access, process or remember information.

It is a limitation to recognise, understand, interpret or respond to information. It can be due to developmental disabilities, brain injury, **alzheimer's[1] disease** or even mental illness.

This type of disability can also be called as **invisible disability** because unlike other disabilities, a person may not be able to assess the condition by just looking at the individual.

It is related to impairments in intellectual functioning and adaptive behaviour. Intellectual functioning means person's ability to plan, comprehend and reason while adaptive behaviour refers to applying social and practical skills in everyday life.

---

1 Alzheimer's This disease is a progressive neurologic disorder that causes the brain shrunk and brain cells to die.

Children suffering from **dyslexia, learning difficulties, speech** disorders, **problem in solving mathematical calculations, short span of attention** and **short of memory** are said to have cognitive disability.

Symptoms of Cognitive Disability

The symptoms of cognitive disability are as follows

- Difficulty in planning and sequencing thoughts and actions.
- Difficulty in interpreting the meaning of numbers and symbols.
- Emotional imbalances or/and emotional outbursts.
- Motor coordination not proper, poor posture or physical imbalance.
- Difficulty in learning and memorising.

Intellectual Disability

Intellectual disability is a disability characterised by significant limitations in both intellectual functioning and adaptive behaviour. This disability originates before the age of 18.

The nature of this disability is also mental since the intellectual domain is related to using the capacity of mind. It is a disability characterised by significant limitations in both personal and social behaviour.

This is characterised by low **Intelligence Quotient** (IQ) score (under 70) and significant problems in the ways learners adapt to new situations.

Symptoms of Intellectual Disability

The symptoms of intellectual disability are as follows

- Very little interpersonal skills.
- Not understanding or following rules and instructions.
- Lack of practical skills like activities of daily living, personal care, etc.
- Reduced capacity to learn, solve problems and reasoning.

Difference between Cognitive and Intellectual Disability

Cognitive disability and intellectual disability may seem the same but there are lots of differences between the two which are as follows

- Cognitive disability is more related to weaknesses in certain academic skills like in reading, writing or calculations. It is also known as 'learning difficulty', while, intellectual disability is also known as 'learning disability' and described as below average IQ along with lack of skills needed for daily living.
- Cognitive disability affects only a certain specific part of the mind. The child performs all the other activities properly. However, intellectual disability is more severe in nature as the child is not able to perform even the daily activities along with difficulty in learning.

Physical Disability

Physical disability is the long-term loss or impairment of a body part that limits the body's physical function. A person with physical disability cannot perform many actions independently.

It may be a motor deficiency or a sensory impairment. Motor deficiency is related to spinal cord, causing paralysis to some or all parts of the body. It may also lead to brain damage, which may occur before or after birth or after a stroke.

On the other hand, sensory impairment is related to an individual's visual or hearing impairments.

The nature of this disability is physical as it is related to physical functioning of the body parts including sense organs.

This refers to the limitation on a person's **physical functioning, mobility, dexterity** or **stamina.**

This includes upper or lower limb loss, poor manual dexterity, visual impairment, hearing loss or disability in coordination with different organs of the body.

Apart from these, **blindness, respiratory disorders, epilepsy**[2] and sleep disorders are also considered as physical disability.

Symptoms of Physical Disability

The symptoms of physical disability are as follows

- Lack of mobility in any part of the body.
- Problems related to senses such as sight, hearing or speech impairment.
- Lack of motor skills and missing developmental milestones.
- Lack of control of the limbs or other body parts.

Causes of Disability

There are various causes of disability which are discussed as follows

1. **Accidents** A wide variety of disabilities, especially those associated with traumatic brain injury result from vehicular accidents, burns, etc.

   Workplace accidents, especially in less regulated sectors such as construction, agriculture, mining and smaller businesses are also a common source of disability.

2. **Poverty** It is one of the biggest causes of disability. Poor people are most vulnerable to disability because they are forced to live and work in unsafe environment with poor sanitation, crowded living conditions and with little access to education, clean water or nutritious food. This gives rise to various diseases such as tuberculosis, polio etc.

---

2 Epilepsy It is a central nervous system (neurological) disorder in which brain activity becomes abnormals.

3. **War** Land mines, cluster bombs, bullets and chemicals used in wars cause more disabilities in the world today than anything else.

   Explosions cause people to become deaf, blind and lose their limbs, as well as causing other injuries. Their mental health is also affected by such violence.

4. **Nuclear Accidents** Many people have suffered after being exposed to massive amounts of radiation. One of the incident that we can refer is when USA dropped nuclear bombs on Japan in 1945. This incident caused widespread destruction and death from exposure to radiation.

   The people who survived these accidents and bombing attacks have suffered mainly from cancer and tumors in various body parts of the body, especially in the thyriod gland or leukemia, all of which causes an early death.

5. **Poor Access to Healthcare** Good health care can prevent various disabilities. Trained birth attendants who can identify risks and handle emergencies, can prevent babies from being born with many disabilities.

   Immunisation can also prevent many disabilities. But many times, vaccines are not available or people who are poor or live far from cities cannot afford them or there are not enough facilities available for everyone, which leads to various disabilities.

6. **Inherited Disabilities** Disabilities also pass from one generation to another. Such disabilities are referred as inherited disabilities. These are also known as genetic disabilities.

   Some disabilities are known to be inherited, such as spinal muscular atrophy *i.e.* diseases of muscles and of nerve cells that carry signals from the brain to the muscle, making the muscles of the body get weaker and weaker and slowly stop working.

7. **Illness** Illness is one of the most important factors of disabilities. There are various causes of illness such as virus, bacteria, pathogens, etc.

   For instance, illness of a pregnant woman can cause birth defect to her baby also. Some illnesses can also cause disability, such as **Meningitis**, **Polio** and **Measles**. It is important for newborn babies to get immunisation for protection.

8. **Malnutrition** It is one of the major causes of disability, especially witnessed in our country. Malnutrition and under nutrition in older adults can also increase the likelihood of breaking of bones, including hip fractures, which can lead to limited physical mobility.

   Micro nutrient and macro nutrient deficiencies are risk factors for physical, sensory and cognitive impairment.

9. **Poisons and Pesticides** Poison such as lead found in paints or pesticides found in various products can cause disabilities in people and cause birth defects in babies growing in the womb.

   Smoking or chewing tobacco, inhaling smoke and drinking alcohol during pregnancy can also harm a child before he/she is born.

10. **Medicines and Vaccines** Both medicines and vaccines are essential to protect health and prevent disability, but there are number of practitioners in the medical field who are not qualified or registered. They don't take proper care while dealing with patients.

    The use of unclean syringes may cause serious diseases like Hepatitis or HIV/AIDS. Improperly stored as well as wrong vaccines may cause allergic reactions, poisoning and deafness to the child.

11. **Dangerous Working Conditions** If individuals are working in factories, mines or agricultural fields under improper working conditions, they may be exposed to dangerous machinery, tools or chemicals and wide variety of health hazards. In such conditions, they may get disabilities in the long-run.

Concept of Disorder

Disorder is an ailment that disturbs the health of a person, hinders a person's performance and diminishes his/her efficiency. Disorder changes the behaviours, thoughts and emotions that may cause significant distress to either self or others.

A person with a disorder, is not able to meet his personal needs on his own or is at a danger to himself or to others. Disorder grows inside a person. It is small in the beginning, but may become serious and grow into a disability.

According to **Medical Journal,** "Disorder is a significant behavioural or psychological syndrome or pattern that occurs in an individual and is associated with present distress or increased risk of suffering of self or others."

There are many kinds of disorders like mental disorder, neurological disorder, hyper activity disorder, eating disorder, addiction disorder, attention disorder, etc.

Regular exercise reduces the incidence of disorders by preventing risk factors which cause impairment. Physical education increases mental concentration and improves functional fitness.

Types of Disorder, Its Causes and Nature

A disorder is referred to as a disturbance in physical or mental health or lack of certain functions of the body that causes dysfunction.

Some types of disorders are discussed as follows

ADHD (Attention Deficit Hyperactivity Disorder)

Attention Deficit Hyperactivity Disorder (ADHD) is a common childhood behavioural disorder characterised by persistent pattern of inattention, hyperactivity, impulsivity that occurs in academic or social settings.

It is basically a condition that affects how well one can focus, sit still or pay attention.

The nature of this disorder is related to behavioural changes or disorders. About 10% of school going kids suffer from ADHD.

Boys are more suspectible to this disorder than girls. Children with ADHD may understand what's expected by them but have trouble in following the instructions, required to complete the task.

Young children mostly act in this way when they are excited or anxious, but the difference with ADHD is that the symptoms are present in a kid suffering from longer period of time and takes place in different settings.

The ADHD disorder affects a child's academic performance as well as social behaviour.

Symptoms of ADHD

The symptoms of ADHD are as follows

- Hyperactivity, excessive talking, impulsivity, difficulty awaiting one's turn.
- Become easily distracted, trouble focusing on a task.
- Very short span of attention, failing to complete tasks.
- Problems staying organised and keeping track of things.
- Mood swings, carelessness and forgetfulness.
- Anxiety attacks, low self-esteem and sleep disorder.

Causes of ADHD

The causes of ADHD are as follows

1. **Genes and Heredity** Genetic inheritance and abnormalities in genes that is acquired by birth, may cause this disorder.
2. **Brain Injury and Epilepsy** Children who have had traumatic brain injuries or who have epilepsy can often have ADHD symptoms.
3. **Environmental Causes** Prenatal exposure to smoke, exposure to high levels of lead as a toddler and preschooler is also a possible contributor.
4. **Lower Birth Weight and Diet** It is observed that children with lower birth weight and intake of specific categories of food or food additives leads to develop ADHD.

SPD (Sensory Processing Disorder)

The Sensory Processing Disorder is a condition in which the brain has trouble in receiving and responding to information that comes in through senses.

Children suffering from SPD are either under-reactive or over-reactive. They also lack motor skills, have short span of attention and delayed communication skills.

The SPD is related to mental nature. The sensory inputs which are not organised by the brain in an appropriate manner, cause SPD. This affects and interferes with the normal everyday functioning of the children.

Children with SPD have delayed communication and social skills. This even affects their self-esteem and as a result, they show poor performance in academics, sports and co-curricular activities.

Their attention span is low and they are not able to concentrate in studies or other activities. Thus, the lack of sensory coordination interferes with the overall functioning of the children.

Symptoms of SPD

The symptoms of SPD are as follows

- Showing heightened reactivity to sound, touch, taste or movement.
- Under-reactive in certain situations e.g. not noticing when name is called.
- Lethargic, disinterested, poor motor skills, lack of attention, impulsive behaviours, etc.

Causes of SPD

1. **Genetic Factors** Genetic or hereditary factors such as having a family history of **autism** or SPD.
2. **Neurological Issue** Understimulation during critical periods of neurological development may develop SPD in that child.
3. **Allergic Issue** Allergy to certain type of foods may cause different reactions leading to disorders.
4. **Environmental Toxins** Childrens' constant exposure to a variety of environmental toxins may also cause SPD.
5. **Abnormal Development** Developmental delays and other neurological disorders like slow sensory reaction may cause SPD.

ASD (Autism Spectrum Disorder)

Autism Spectrum Disorder is a serious developmental disorder that impairs the ability to communicate and interact.

It is neurodevelopmental condition that affects the brain's growth and development. It is a lifelong condition and the symptoms appear in early childhood.

The nature of this disorder is related to mental illness which then changes the behaviour. It is a complex developmental disorder that affects normal brain development.

People with ASD, face difficulty in communication and social interaction with people. They also have repetitive behaviour patterns like flicking a light switch repeatedly, smelling everything, flipping objects, etc.

Children with ASD also have sensory sensitivities such as not using eye contact, confused in how to express in words, repeating a word often, etc. Here, the brain does not function in the typical way due to which they face developmental challenges.

Symptoms of ASD

The symptoms of ASD are as follows

- Children and adults with ASD do not acquire good social skills.
- Face many behavioural problems.
- Often stare at a particular person or object and may like a few foods only.
- Get over-excited by certain sounds, etc.

Causes of ASD

The Causes of ASD are as follows

1. **Genetic Factors** ASD can be the result of heredity factors, genetic differences and genetic mutations. ASD is more common in boys than girls as it is most likely linked to genetic differences associated with the X-chromosome.

2. **Abnormal Brain Development** It can also cause through abnormal brain development and other neurobiological factors.

   One of the symptomatic behaviours include disruptions in normative patterns of social neuro- development that contribute to diminished attention to social stimuli.

3. **Environmental Factors** Factors related to exposure to drugs, toxins like lead, insecticides, hydrocarbons and dietary factors may cause ASD.

ODD (Oppositional Defiant Disorder)

Oppositional Defiant Disorder is a type of disorder that is marked by defiant and disobedient behaviour to authority figures like parents, teachers, guardians, etc.

The nature of this disorder is related to social behaviour. This behaviour disorder usually takes place in early teens. Apart from teens, ODD also affects young children, especially boys.

In children, it begins from the age of 8 years. About 2-16% of children are affected by ODD.

Due to ODD, children in their early teens, try to defy authority every now and then, they express their defiance by arguing, disobeying, talking back to parents, teachers and other adults. They may often behave this way when they are tired, hungry or upset due to stress.

Though this type of behaviour is normally seen among all the teenagers, but the difference in ODD is that the behaviour lasts more than 6 months and is excessive in one child in comparison to other child of the same age. This kind of behaviour often disrupts the child's normal daily activities and hampers academic performance.

Symptoms of ODD

The symptoms of ODD are as follows

- Similar patterns of anger.
- Irritable mood.
- Argumentative or defiant behaviour.
- Flaring up at trivial matters.
- Saying hateful things and seeking revenge.

Causes of ODD

The causes of ODD are as follows

1. **Genetics** It is common for children, who are diagnosed with ODD, to have family members who also suffer from various mental illnesses. Such illnesses can include **mood disorders**, **personality disorders** and **anxiety disorders**.

   This fact suggests that there is most likely a genetic component that leads a person to be more suspectible to develop ODD, as opposed to a person who has not been exposed to the next type of genetics.

2. **Environmental** Similarly, if children are exposed to violence or have friends who behave in destructive, reckless manners, those children too are more likely to begin displaying behavioural symptoms that correlate with the onset of ODD.

3. **Physical** The presence of ODD traits have been linked to the existence of abnormal amount of certain brain chemicals.

   These brain chemicals, known as neuro transmitters, helps in proper functioning of body activities, thus they should remain in balanced state in our brain.

   When an imbalance exists, and messages are suddenly unable to communicate properly with other aspects of the brain, symptoms of ODD may occur.

ODD (Oppositional Defiant Disorder) in Adults

Adults with Oppositional Defiant Disorder (ODD) display a pattern of negative, hostile and defiant behaviour that lasts for atleast six months.

Adults with ODD are more than just aggressive and irritating from time to time. They defend themselves relentlessly when someone says they have done something wrong. They see themselves as mistreated, misunderstood and unappreciated always.

Symptoms of ODD in Adults

- Often loses temper
- Often argues with family and co-workers
- Deliberately annoys people
- Easily annoyed by others
- Spiteful or vindictive

OCD (Obsessive Compulsive Disorder)

Obsessive Compulsive Disorder (OCD) is a mental health condition that revolves around a **debilitating obsession** or **compulsion, distressing** actions and **repetitive thoughts**. The person feels the need to repeat the behaviours over and over.

The nature of this disorder is related to mental illness. Males and females both are equally affected by OCD. About 15-20% of the people experience OCD in mild forms.

People doing repetative behaviours, performing routine tasks over an over again or having certain thoughts repeatedly are said to have OCD.

Some examples of this type of disorder are frequent or excessive hand washing, counting things repeatedly, checking if door is locked again and again.

These activities occur to such a degree that it affects a person's life negatively.

OCD is associated with a wide range of functional impairments and has a significant impact on social and working life.

Symptoms of OCD

The symptoms of OCD are as follows

- Fear of being contaminated by germs or dirt or contaminating others.
- Aggressive thoughts towards others or self.
- Habitual of doing or having things in a perfect order always.
- Repeatedly checking things and compulsive counting.
- Spending a considerable time in a day on their thoughts and behaviours.
- A fear of being embarrassed.

Causes of OCD

The causes of OCD are as follows

1. **Familial Disorder** If parents or other family members are suffering from OCD, then other individuals of the family are likely to develop it. It is also inherited from one generation to another. Hence, it is genetic in nature.

   Twin studies of adults suggest that obsessive compulsive symptoms are moderately inherited, with genetic factors contributing 27 to 47 per cent variance in scores that measure obsessive compulsive symptoms.

2. **Behavioural Causes** The Behavioural Theory suggests that people with OCD associate certain objects or situations with fear and learn to avoid those things or learn to perform 'rituals' in order to help reduce the fear or the stress related to that situation.

   This fear and avoidance or ritual cycle may begin during a period of intense stress, such as when starting a new job.

3. **Cognitive Causes** This happens when people misinterpret their thoughts like the feeling of dirty hands even when they are cleaned many times.

   Most people can shrug-off and disregard the thought, but a person with OCD may exaggerate the importance of the thought and respond as though it signifies a threat.

   For example, a person who is caring for an infant and who is under intense pressure may have an intrusive thought of harming the infant either deliberately or accidentally.

4. **Environmental Causes** This means stressful situation present in the environment such as within the family or society that triggers OCD in people.

Disability Etiquettes

Disability etiquette is a set of guidelines that explain how to approach or how to deal with the people facing physical or mental disabilities. The term serves to communicate people with disabilities more respectfully in all types of situations.

It refers to educate people regarding disabilities. It involves treating people with disabilities with respect and care, and try to bring them into a normal life. There is no certain time period as to when it started, but it is believed to come into existence in 1970.

The **Disability Rights Movement** that came around in the same period is said to divert the attention of the world towards disabled people. As part of Civil Rights, it was felt necessary to write about disability etiquettes in order to understand and respect the disabled people.

Disability Etiquettes in General

The rules of etiquette for the disabled people are generally the same as the rules for good etiquette in society. The disability etiquettes are as follows

- It is always important to respect the dignity of disabled people. So, talk to them with respect so that their self-esteem and confidence is built up.
- When introduced to a person with disability, it is appropriate to offer shake hands.
- Never patronise people who use wheelchairs by patting them on the head or shoulder.
- Respect the individuality of the person. So, avoid generalising the disabled people and call them by their names.
- Talk to the person and address him/her directly instead of talking through a friend or an interpreter who may also be present.
- If you offer assistance, wait until the person responds. Then, listen carefully to his/her instructions.
- Do not speak about the disabled people as if they are invisible or cannot understand what is being said.
- Do not show extra attention or added care as it may give a feeling of sympathy. Treat them with the same attention and care as with normal people.
- Respect the privacy of the person. Do not ask unnecessary questions about the disability or how they are coping with it.
- When people with disability ask for any assistance, respond to it graciously.

Disability Etiquette Guidelines

Apart from general guidelines, the etiquette guidelines can also be classified according to the different types of disabilities. The disability etiquette guidelines for people with speech difficulties, hearing loss, vision loss, cognitive impairments and mobility impairments are discussed below

Persons with Speech Difficulties

- Give attention to the person who has difficulty in speaking.
- Keep your manner encouraging rather than correcting.
- Give extra time for the conversation with these people and be patient.

- If you have difficulty in understanding, don't pretend that you do. Repeat as much as you do understand.
- Use short sentences with simple and concrete words.

Persons with Hearing Loss

- Get the person's attention with a wave of the hand, or a tap on the shoulder.
- Speak clearly and slowly, but without exaggerating your lip movements or shouting.
- Many persons with hearing loss read lips. Place yourself facing the light source and keep hands, cigarettes and food away from your mouth while talking, in order to provide a clear view of your face.
- When an interpreter accompanies a person, direct your remarks to the person rather than to the interpreter.
- Look directly at the person and speak expressively.
- Use sign language if you and the person are familiar with it.

Persons with Vision Loss

- When you enter a room, indicate who you are. Let the person know when you are leaving the room.
- Remember that you will need to communicate any written information orally.
- When talking to a person with a visual impairment, begin identifying yourself by name and that you are speaking to them.
- When offering your assistance, do not grab a person's cane or arm.
- If you are walking with a person who is blind, offer your arm for him to hold.
- Walk at the normal pace. It is helpful to speak casually and naturally about the environment, objects and buildings you are passing as you walk.
- Not all visually impaired people read Braille. Ask the person what alternative format they prefer.

Persons with Cognitive/Language Impairment

- Use a calm voice and be comfortable. Use simple and short sentences.
- Do not argue with the person.
- Treat each person as an individual with talents and abilities, deserving of respect and dignity.
- Give extra time for the person to process what you are saying and to respond.
- Look for signs of stress and/or confusion.
- Keep your manner encouraging rather than correcting.

Persons with Mobility Impairment

Mobility impairment means difficulty in movement. To cope up with this difficulty, wheelchairs, walking sticks and several other things are used.

The disability etiquettes for mobility impairment are as follows

- Don't push, pull or touch the wheelchair, walking sticks or other objects that the person might be using.
- Be aware of the person's reach limits. For that, place the item where it is easily reachable.
- Be prepared to offer assistance to the disabled people with reaching, grasping or lifting objects, opening doors, operating vending machines and other equipments.
- Step down or bend to enquire about the person who is sitting on a wheelchair.

The rules of etiquettes and good manners to deal with people with disabilities, generally focus on treating the disabled people with respect and care as well as acknowledging their individuality.

These guidelines address specific issues which frequently arise for people with disabilities.

Physical Activities for Children with Special Needs (CWSN)

According to the **Department of Health and Human Services** (USA), "physical activity generally refers to movement that enhances health".

Physical activity means the movement of the body that uses energy. Walking, running, dancing, swimming, yoga and gardening are few examples of physical activity.

For health benefits, physical activity should be of moderate intensity. It can be vigorous also, if more amount of activities are to be done.

Regular physical activity is good for everyone but it's particularly important for children with special needs. Infact, regular physical activities result in improved functional status and quality of life among children with special needs.

Strategies to Make Physical Activities Assessable for CWSN

Doing regular exercises and lot of physical activities keeps one physically fit and fine. In case of children with special needs, physical activities are like blessings.

They bring physical and mental development along with developing self-esteem, confidence and interpersonal skills. Therefore, it is essential to include physical activities in the daily life of children with special needs.

The various strategies or ways by which physical activities can be made assessable for children with special needs are as follows

1. **Medical Check-up** If we want to make physical activities accessible for the children with special needs, we need to understand the type of disabilities of children and for this purpose, complete medical check-up of the children is required.

   It is essential because without a complete medical chek-up, the teachers of physical education will face difficulty in knowing about the type of disability the child is facing.

2. **Assistive Technology** It refers to creating devices, tools or equipments that help children with special needs to participate in learning activities, like bigger balls, balls with bells, balls attached to strings to bring it back to the students, etc.

   If normal schools develop adequate infrastructure to support the activities of children with special needs, then parents of these children can get their child admitted in any school.

3. **Adaptive Physical Education** It means developing, implementing and monitoring a carefully designed physical education instructional programme for a learner with disability. For this, various changes have to be made.

   Depending on student's disability, a separate, adaptive class or modifications within a game, changing the rules of the game or sport to some extent can help the student in a great way.

4. **Creating Specific Environment** This means making a friendly atmosphere by keeping in mind the specific needs of the children with disability.

   In this way, it shows that they are also wanted in society and like other children of their age, they can also play.

   Students with special needs can be provided with specific play area with special requirements as needed by them.

   For example, loud music, glaring lights often cannot be tolerated by these children, so lot of natural lighting should be there.

5. **Activities Based on Interests** Physical activities must be based on interests, aptitudes, abilities, previous experiences and limitations of children with special needs.

The teachers of physical education should have deep knowledge of limitations, interests and aptitudes of children, which will help them to make physical activities accessible for children with special needs easily.

6. **Different Instructional Strategies** A variety of different instructional strategies like verbal, visual and peer teaching should be used for performing various types of physical activities. By this, children get the opportunity to learn on their own and become independent.

7. **Modification of Rules** Rules can be modified according to the needs of the children. They can be provided extra time or attempt to perform a physical activity.

   They can also be given extra time to rest before doing next physical activity, etc.

8. **Professional Courses** Developing more professional courses and teacher certification programmes for teaching physical education to children with special needs is essential to popularise the adaptive physical education programmes. Special education degree programmes and many diploma courses are available, nowadays.

   However, more such programmes need to be developed at the university level and students should be encouraged to take up these courses.

9. **Children's Previous Experience must be Taken into Consideration** For making physical activities more accessible for children with special needs, the concerned teacher of physical education should have comprehensive understanding and knowledge of children's pervious experience about physical activities. He/she should make proper arrangement of equipments, considering such experience and comfortability of children.

Chapter Practice

Objective Questions

• Multiple Choice Questions

1. Cognitive disability is a broad term that includes **(CBSE 2020)**

(a) Intellectual disability   (b) Locomotor disability
(c) Speech impairment   (d) All of these

Ans. (a) Cognitive disability is a broader term that includes intellectual disability.

2. Emotional imbalances or emotional outbursts are the symptoms of ________ .

(a) Intellectual disability   (b) Cognitive disability
(c) Physical disability   (d) None of these

Ans. (b) Emotional imbalances or emotional outbursts are the symptoms of cognitive disability. Cognitive disability is related to sudden sadness, anger etc. It affects the adaptive behaviour of the children due to which they experience emotional imbalances.

3. The class teacher of VII-A observed newly joined student Sekhar's behaviour. He is different from other students. He has difficulty in thinking and understanding concepts taught at school. The class teacher called his parents and suggested them to take him to a psychologist.

The person with intellectual disability has IQ between

(a) 70-75%   (b) 80-85%   (c) 85-90%   (d) 90-95%

Ans. (a) The person with intellectual disability has IQ between 70-75%. IQ test means the level of intelligence of an individual.

4. Identify the type of disability shown in the picture.

(a) Intellectual disability   (b) Physical disability
(c) Cognitive disability   (d) None of these

Ans. (b) The type of disability shown in the image is physical disability as the boy is sitting on a wheelchair. This means that the lower portion of the body cannot perform its function independently.

5. ADHD means **(CBSE 2020)**

(a) Automatic Deficit Hyperactivity Disorder
(b) Attention Deficit Hyperactivity Disorder
(c) Attention Deficit Hyperactivity
(d) None of the above

Ans. (b) ADHD means Attention Deficit Hyperactivity Disorder. It is characterised by persistent pattern of intention, hyperactivity, impulsivity that occurs in academic or social settings.

6. A 6 year old boy is so hyperactive and talkative in class that the teacher, find it very difficult to assign a task for him. Based on this, answer the following.

The boy is likely to suffer from
(a) SPD
(b) ODD
(c) ASD
(d) ADHD

Ans. (d) The boy is likely to suffer from ADHD. Hyperactivity, talkative, failure to complete a task and Very short span of attention are all characteristics of ADHD.

7. Seetha who is studying in class XI at Kaveri School has a tendency to forget things along with a flickering mind. She is also not able to sit quietly in a place for a while. The teacher observed her and advised Seetha's parents during a parent teacher meeting to meet a counsellor.

ADHD is most common among ________ .
(a) Male   (b) Female
(c) Children   (d) None of these

Ans. (c) ADHD is most common among children.

8. Shruti joined as a teacher in a school that caters to students with special needs. The principal explained her about the special needs of the children and also about disability etiquettes.

Most suitable word used for disable person is ___.
(a) Disabled person   (b) Retarded
(c) Divyang   (d) Blind

Ans. (c) Most suitable word used for disable person is divyang

9. Regular physical exercise results in _______.
(a) Improved functional status
(b) Quality of life
(c) Improved cognitive abilities
(d) All of the above

Ans. (d) Regular physical exercise results in improved functional status, quality of life and improved cognitive abilities.

10. SPD means
(a) Special Police Department
(b) Sensory Processing Disorder
(c) Special Processing Disorder
(d) Sensory Protecting Disorder

Ans. (b) SPD means Sensory Processing Disorder. It is a condition in which the brain has trouble in receiving and responding to information that comes in through senses.

11. Children who are not cooperative, defiant and disrespectful towards elders are diagnosed with
(a) ODD   (b) OCD   (c) SPD   (d) ADHD

Ans. (a) Children who are not cooperative, defiant and disrespectful towards elders are diagnosed with ODD.

12. Disability etiquette means _______ .
(a) Educating normal people regarding disabilities.
(b) Treating disabled people with care and respect.
(c) Both (a) and (b)
(d) None of the above

Ans (c) Disability etiquette means educating normal people regarding disabilities and treating disabled people with care and respect.

13. Match the following.

	List I		List II
A.	Cognitive	1.	Strategies or plans
B.	OCD	2.	Etiquettes
C.	Sympathy	3	Disorder
D.	Physical activities	4.	Disability
E.	Medical check-up	5.	Improves fitness

Codes

	A	B	C	D	E			A	B	C	D	E
(a)	1	2	3	4	5		(b)	2	1	3	5	4
(c)	4	3	2	5	1		(d)	3	4	5	1	2

Ans. (c) The correct match is A-4, B-3, C-2, D-5, E-1

14. Match the following.

	List I		List II
A	ADHD	1.	Argumentative or defiant behaviour
B.	SPD	2.	Get overexcited by certain sounds
C.	ASD	3.	Underreactive in certain situations
D.	ODD	4.	Fear of being contaminated by germs or dirt or contaminating others
E.	OCD	5.	Very short span of attention, failing to complete tasks

Codes

	A	B	C	D	E			A	B	C	D	E
(a)	1	2	3	4	5		(b)	5	3	2	1	4
(c)	3	2	4	1	5		(d)	5	4	3	2	1

Ans. (b) The correct match is A-5, B-3, C-2, D-1, E-4

15. Ravi is a new student in Rakesh sir's class. His behaviour is different from other students, he is aggressive, rude and uncooperative, he finds it difficult to make friends in school nobody wants to be his friend. Rakesh discussed this situation with his classmates and told them about ODD.

ODD patients do not show sign of
(a) Anger   (b) Calmness
(c) Vindictiveness   (d) Irritation

Ans. (b) ODD patients do not show signs of calmness. In fact, they are opposite of being calm. They show anger, irritation and vindictiveness.

• Assertion and Reasoning

Directions (Q.Nos. 1-4) *Each of these questions contains two statements, Assertion (A) and Reason (R). Each of these questions also has four alternative choices, any one of which is the correct answer. You have to select one of the codes (a), (b), (c) and (d) given below.*

Codes
(a) Both A and R are true and R is the correct explanation of A
(b) Both A and R are true, but R is not the correct explanation of A
(c) A is true, but R is false
(d) A is false, but R is true

1. **Assertion** (A) Disability affects a person's life in many ways.

Reason (R) Disability is multi-dimensional concept.

Ans. (a) Assertion is true as disability affects a person's life in many ways like by physical, cognitive or intellectual way. Disability has lot of aspects, so it is multidimensional. Reason explains assertion so correctly. Thus, both A and R are true and R is the correct explanation of A.

2. Assertion (A) Genetic conditions cause genetic mutations that may result in intellectual disability.

Reason (R) Down syndrome is a genetic condition that may lead to intellectual disability.

Ans. (b) Assertion is true as genetic condition is one of the factors that may cause intellectual disability.

Reason is also true as Down syndrome is a genetic condition that is one of the causes of intellectual disability. Thus, both A and R are true and R is not the correct explanation of A.

3. Assertion (A) Obsessive Compulsive Disorder is a type of mental disorder.

Reason (R) People do repetitive behaviours or perform tasks repeatedly.

Ans. (a) Assertion is true as OCD is a type of disorder that affects the mental health of a person. Reason is also true as a person do repetitive behaviours. Here reason explains assertion properly. Thus, both A and R are true and R is the correct explanation of A.

4. Assertion (A) For health benefits, physical activity should be of moderate intensity.

Reason (R) Regular physical activity resulted in improved functional status and quality of life among children with special needs.

Ans. (b) Assertion is true as moderate intensity of physical activity provides lot of health benefits. Reason is also true as children with special need become active, social and fit by doing regular physical activities. Thus, both A and R are true, but R is not the correct explanation of A.

• Case Based MCQs

1. School management needs to recognise the essential place of physical activity in the education of children with special needs. In order to develop lifelong habits for fitness and to provide them with many opportunities of socialisation, schools need to understand that physical education is not a secondary subject but it is just as important as other skills. **(CBSE Question Bank 2021)**

(i) Which of these is not one of the results of physical activities in children with special needs?
(a) Improvement in confidence
(b) Improvement in endurance
(c) Increase in depression
(d) Better hand-eye coordination

Ans. (c) Increase in depression is not the result of physical activity in children withspecial needs.

(ii) Match the following.

	List I		List II
A.	Cognitive	1.	Disorder
B.	OCD	2.	Improvement techniques
C.	Physical activities	3.	Disability
D.	Competition in sports and games for CWSN	4.	Paralympics

Codes

	A	B	C	D
(a)	3	1	2	4
(b)	4	2	1	3
(c)	2	3	4	1
(d)	4	3	1	2

Ans. (a) The correct match is A-3, B-1, C-2, D-4.

(iii) Name the model which refers to bringing students with disabilities and students of general education into the same platform of learning.
(a) Inclusive education
(b) UNESCO
(c) Child Rights and You
(d) Child Rights International Network

Ans. (a) Inclusive education bringing student into the same platform of learning.

2. Ankit is in class X recently he has developed the habit of arguing disobeying and talking back to parents, teachers and guardians. Based on this information, answer the following questions.

(i) A pattern of disobedience can be observed in children suffering from
(a) ODD (b) OCD
(c) SPD (d) ADHD

Ans. (a) A pattern of disobedience can be observed in children suffering from ODD.

(ii) Expended form of ODD is
(a) Opposite different disorder
(b) Oppositional deficient disorder
(c) Opposite different disability
(d) Obsessive defect disability

Ans. (b) Oppositional deficient disorder is the expanded form of ODD.

(iii) The cause for this disorder can be
(a) indiscipline (b) family environment
(c) Both (a) and (b) (d) accident

Ans. (c) The causes for this disorder can be indiscipline and family environment.

PART 2

Subjective Questions

• Short Answer (SA) Type Questions

1. What are the types of disability? Explain briefly.
(**CBSE 2018**)

Ans. Disability is of three types, which are as follows

(i) **Cognitive Disability** It is a disability that impacts on individual's ability to access, process or remember information. It is a limitation to recognise, understand, interpret or respond to information.

(ii) **Intellectual Disability** It is a disability characterised by significant limitations in both intellectual functioning and adaptive behaviour. It is more severe in nature as the child is not able to perform even the daily activities along with difficulty in learning.

(iii) **Physical Disability** It is a long-term loss or impairment of a body part that limits the body's physical function. A person with physical disability cannot perform many actions independently. It may be a motor deficiency or a sensory impairment.

2. Write any three causes of disability.

Ans. Three causes of disability are discussed as follows

(i) **Accidents** A wide variety of disabilities especially those associated with traumatic brain injury result from vehicular accidents, burns, falls etc.

(ii) **Poverty** It is one of the biggest causes of disability. Poor people are most vulnerable to disability because they are forced to live and work in unsafe environment with poor sanitation, crowded living conditions and with little access to education, clear water or enough good food.

(iii) **War** Land mines, cluster bombs, bullets and chemicals used in wars, cause more disabilities in the world today than anything else.

3. Explain the condition of Attention Deficit Hyperactivity Disorder.

Ans. ADHD is basically a condition that affects how well one can focus, sit still or pay attention.

The nature of this disorder is related to behavioural changes or disorders. About 10% of school going kids suffer from ADHD.

Boys are more suspectible to this disorder than girls. Children with ADHD may understand what's expected by them but have trouble in following the instructions, required to complete the task.

Young children mostly act in this way when they are excited or anxious, but the difference with ADHD is that the symptoms are present in a kid suffering from longer period of time and takes place in different settings.

The ADHD disorder affects a child's academic performance as well as social behaviour.

4. Explain the symptoms of ADHD.

Ans. Symptoms of ADHD are as follows

• Hyperactivity, excessive talking, impulsivity, difficulty awaiting one's turn.

• Become easily distracted, trouble focusing on a task.

• Very short span of attention, failing to complete tasks.

• Problems staying organised and keeping track of things.

• Mood swings, carelessness and forgetfulness.

• Anxiety attacks, low self-esteem and sleep disorder.

5. Elaborate the causes that lead to ADHD (Attention Deficit Hyperactivity Disorder) and SPD (Sensory Processing Disorder).

Ans. The causes leading to the two disorders are as follows

ADHD Causes

(i) **Genes and Heredity** Genetic inheritance and abnormalities in genes that is acquired from birth, may cause this disorder.

(ii) **Brain Injury and Epilepsy** Children who have had traumatic brain injuries or who have epilepsy can often have ADHD symptoms.

SPD Causes

(i) **Neurological ISSUE** Understimulated during critical periods of neurological development.

(ii) **Genetic factor** Genetic or heredity factors such as having a history of autism or SPD.

6. How does the Sensory Processing Disorder interferes with a child's normal everyday functioning?

Ans. The Sensory Processing Disorder is a condition in which the brain has trouble in receiving and responding to information that comes in through senses. Children suffering from SPD are either under-reactive or over-reactive.

They also lack motor skills, have short span of attention and delayed communication skills.

Due to these symptoms, the children with SPD are not able to concentrate in studies or other activities. So the lack of sensory coordination with the brain in an appropriate manner interferes with the children's normal everyday functioning.

7. Write a short note on ASD.

Ans. **Autism Spectrum Disorder** (ASD) is a type of mental disorder that impairs the ability to communicate and interact. It is a developmental disorder that affects normal brain functioning.

People with ASD have repetitive behaviour patterns like flicking a light switch repeatedly, flipping objects etc. Causes of ASD are as follows

　(i) **Genetic Factors** It can be the result of heredity factors, genetic differences and genetic mutations.

　(ii) **Abnormal Brain Development** It can also cause through abnormal mechanisms of brain development and other neurobiological factors.

8. Explain the strategy of positive behaviour in brief.

Ans. The strategy of positive behaviour relates to showing a positive attitude and having healthy interactions with the children with special needs. The teachers should prevent negative behaviours and encourage these children to participate in classroom activities.

Teachers and parents of children with special needs should encourage more interaction with normal children to develop a proper social behaviour.

9. A child's mother has the habit of washing her hands frequently. What kind of disorder she might be suffering from? Explain with its symptoms.

Ans. Child's mother is suffering from Obsessive Compulsive Disorder (OCD). It is a mental health condition that involves around a debilitating obsession or compulsion, distressing actions and repetitive thoughts. The person feels the need to repeat the behaviours over and over.

The symptoms of OCD are as follows

● Fear of being contaminated by germs or dirt or contaminating others.

● Aggressive thoughts towards others or self.

● Habitual of doing or having things in a perfect order always.

● Repeatedly checking things and compulsive counting.

● Spending a considerable time in a day on their thoughts and behaviours.

● A fear of being embarrassed.

10. What do you understand by the term disability? Explain any four disability etiquettes.　　**(CBSE 2020)**

Ans Disability means any kind of impairment or permanent reduction in physical or mental capacity of an individual.

It can be a physical loss, mental illness or reduction in the use of sense organs.

Four methods of following disability etiquette are as follows

　(i) Treating disabled people with care and respect.

　(ii) Educating normal people regarding disabilities.

　(iii) Speak directly to the disabled person rather than through friend, attendant or sign-language interpretor, who may also be present.

　(iv) Never speak about the disabled person as if the person is invisible or can't understand what is being said.

11. List the disability etiquettes when dealing with a person who has speech difficulties.

Ans. Disability etiquettes for dealing with a person who has speech difficulties are as follows

● Give attention to the person who has difficulty in speaking.

● Maintain a manner so as to encourage rather than correct.

● Give extra time for the conversation with these people and be patient.

● If you have difficulty in understanding, do not pretend that you do. Repeat as much as you do understand.

12. List the disability etiquettes when dealing with a person with vision loss.

Ans. The etiquettes followed when dealing with a person with vision loss are as follows

● If you are walking with a person who is blind, offer your arm for him to hold.

● Walk at the normal pace. It is helpful to speak casually and naturally about the environment, objects and buildings you are passing as you walk.

● Not all visually impaired people read Braille. Ask the person what alternative format they prefer.

● Long Answer (LA) Type Questions

1. Explain physical disability and its symptoms in detail.

Ans. Physical disability is the long-term loss or impairment of a body part that limits the body's physical function. A person with physical disability cannot perform many actions independently.

It may be a motor deficiency or a sensory impairment. Motor deficiency is related to spinal cord, causing paralysis to some or all parts of the body. It may also lead to brain damage, which may occur before or after birth or after a stroke.

On the other hand, sensory impairment is related to an individual's visual or hearing impairments. The nature of this disability is physical as it is related to physical functioning of the body parts including sense organs. This refers to the limitation on a person's **physical functioning, mobility, dexterity** or **stamina**.

This includes upper or lower limb loss, poor manual dexterity, visual impairment, hearing loss or disability in coordination with different organs of the body.

Apart from these, **blindness**, **respiratory disorders**, **epilepsy** and sleep disorders are also considered as physical disability.

Symptoms of Physical Disability

The symptoms of physical disability are as follows

- Lack of mobility in any part of the body.
- Problems related to senses such as sight, hearing or speech impairment.
- Lack of motor skills and missing developmental milestones.
- Lack of control of the limbs or other body parts.

2. Five years old Saurabh is facing difficulty in reading the letters, he gets confused between lower case of b and d. Which disability is he suffering from? Explain.

Ans. Saurabh is suffering from cognitive disability.

Cognitive disability is a disability that impacts an individual's ability to access, process or remember information. It is a limitation to recognise, understand, interpret or respond to information. It can be due to developmental disabilities, brain injury, alzheimer's disease or even mental illness.

This type of disability can also be called as invisible disability because unlike other disabilities, a person may not be able to assess the condition by just looking at the individual. It is related to impairments in intellectual functioning and adaptive behaviour. Intellectual functioning means person's ability to plan, comprehend and reason while adaptive behaviour refers to applying social and practical skills in everyday life.

Children suffering from dyslexia, learning difficulties, speech disorders, problem in solving mathematical calculations, short span of attention and short of memory are said to have cognitive disability.

3. Explain in detail OCD and ODD.

Ans. **Obsessive Compulsive Disorder** (OCD) It is a mental health condition that revolves around an obsession or compulsion, distressing actions and repetitive thoughts. People with OCD carry out routine tasks repeatedly.

Instances of these are excessive hand washing, counting of things repeatedly, checking if a door is locked many times etc.

Causes of OCD are as follows

  (i) **Familial Disorder** If any member of a family is suffering from OCD, then, other members of the family have high chance of developing it. It is also inherited from one generation to another. Hence, it is also genetic in nature.

  (ii) **Behavioural Causes** The behavioural theory suggests that people with OCD associate certain objects or situations with fear and learn to avoid those things or learn to perform rituals in order to help, reduce the tension or the stress related to that situation.

Oppositional Defiant Disorder (ODD) is a behaviour disorder that usually takes place in early teens. ODD is characterised by an irritable mood, anger, argumentative behaviour, disobeying, talking back and mood swings. Teenangers going through ODD face a number of behavioural problems.

Causes of ODD are as follows

  (i) **Genetics** The most likely is genetic component that leads a person to be more susceptible to developing oppositional defiant disorder, as opposed to a person who has not been exposed to the next type of genetics.

  (ii) **Environmental** Similarly, if children are exposed to violence or have friends who behave in destructive, reckless manners, those children too are more likely to begin displaying behavioural symptoms that correlate with the onset of ODD.

  (iii) **Physical** Neurotransmitters, helps in proper functioning of body activities, thus they should remain in imbalance states in our brain when an imbalance exist in our brain the symptoms of ODD may occur.

4. Is it always important to respect the dignity of the disabled people. In this context, explain the disability etiquettes in general.

Ans. Yes, it is essential to respect the dignity of the disabled people.

The disability etiquettes are as follows

- It is always important to respect the dignity of disabled people. So, talk to them with respect so that their self-esteem and confidence is built up.
- Respect the individuality of the person. So avoid generalising the disabled people and call them by their names.
- Talk to the person and address him/her directly instead of talking through a friend or an interpreter who may also be present there.
- If you offer assistance, wait until the person responds. Then listen carefully to his/her instructions.
- Do not speak about the disabled persons as if they are invisible or cannot understand what is being said.
- Do not show extra attention or added care as it may give a feeling of sympathy. Treat them with the same attention and care as with normal people.

5. Elaborate the disability etiquettes of dealing with people facing speech difficulties and language impairment.

Ans. The disability etiquettes for dealing people with speech difficulties and language impairment are mentioned below

- Give attention to the person who has difficulty in speaking.
- Keep manner to encourage rather than correcting.
- Give extra time for the conversation with these people and be patient.
- If you have difficulty in understanding, don't pretend that you do. Repeat as much as you do understand.
- Use a calm voice and be comfortable. Use simple and short sentences.
- Do not argue with the person.
- Treat each person as an individual with talents and abilities deserving of respect and dignity.

6. Explain five strategies to make physical activities accessible for children with special needs.

Or How physical activities are helpful for children with special need? Explain strategies to make physical activities accessable for them. **(CBSE 2020)**

Ans The five strategies to make physical activities accessible for children with special needs are as follows

(i) **Medical Check-up** If we want to make physical activities accessible for the children with special needs, we need to understand the type of disabilities of children and for this purpose complete medical check-up of the children is required.

(ii) **Assistive Technology** It refers to creating devices, tools or equipments that help children with special needs to participate in learning activities like bigger balls, balls with bells, balls attached to strings etc. This kind of new technology makes physical activities accessible for children with special needs.

(iii) **Adaptive Physical Education** Adapted physical education means developing, implementing and monitoring a carefully designed physical education instructional programme for a learner with a disability.

(iv) **Creating Specific Environment** This means making a friendly atmosphere by keeping in mind the specific needs of the children with disability. In this way, it shows that they are also wanted in society and like other children of their age, they can also play.

(v) **Activities based on Interests** Physical activities must be based on interest, aptitudes, abilities, previous experience and limitations of children with special needs, The teachers of physical education should have deep knowledge of limitations, interests and aptitudes of children.

• Case Based Questions

1. Raju, Sheela and Mili visited their new friends living in a centre for children with special needs. On the day before visiting the centre, they held a meeting with their school Physical Education teacher and learnt many guidelines to deal with their special friends at the centre. They were very much excited to meet them knowing how happy their friends would be.

Based on this case answer the following questions.

(i) How kind of disability etiquette help people to interact with differently abled people?

Ans. Disability etiquette provides various guidelines on how to interact with differently abled people. This makes interaction easier and effective.

(ii) When did disability etiquettes came into existence?

Ans. There is no certain time period as to when it started but it is believed to come into existence in 1970.

2. A teacher in a pre-school noticed that a child is not singing along with other children. She is not responding even when her name is called. Then the teacher asked the child to stand next to her and repeat the rhyme along with her, while she prompted and encouraged her. With effort the child was able to sing like other children of her age. Based on this case, answer the following questions.

(i) Which kind of disorder is it? What could have possibly caused this disorder ?

Ans. The disorder is sensory processing disorder. It is a type of disorder in which brain has trouble in receiving and responding. Genetic factors, neurological problems, accidents may have caused this disorder.

(ii) What are the symptoms of the disorder that is selected by you in question.

Ans. The disorder is SPD and its symptoms are trouble in receiving or responding to information, short attention span, delayed communication etc.

3. Rashi's mother has the habit of washing her hands every few minutes and spends her entire day arranging things exactly the way she wants.

(i) How can the disorder of OCD be identified?

Ans. The disorder of OCD can be indentified by seeing various symptoms like repetative behaviours, distressing actions, debilitating obsessions or compulsions.

(ii) How familial disorders cause OCD?

Ans. If parents or family members suffer from OCD, then other family members are also likely to develop it. It may be inherited from one generation to another also.

Chapter Test

Multiple Choice Questions

1. Frequent or excessive washing of hands is a symptom of the disorder known as ....
(a) Obsessive Compulsive Disorder
(b) Oppositional Defiant Disorder
(c) Sensory Processing Disorder
(d) Autism Spectrum Disorder

2. People suffering from ——— , face difficulty in communication and social interaction with people.
(a) Autism Spectrum Disorder (ASD)
(b) Sensory processing disorder (SPD)
(c) Oppositional Defiant disorder (ODD)
(d) Obsessive compulsive disorder (OCD)

3. Find the incorrect statement
(a) Nuclear accidents can increase disabilities
(b) Inherited disabilities pass from one person to other
(c) Poor people are most vulnerable to disability
(d) Traumatic brain injury may result in disability

4. Cognitive disability can also be called invisible disability because unlike other disabilities, a person may not be able to assess the condition by just looking at the individual. It is related to impairments in intellectual functioning and adaptive behaviour.

Based on the identify which of the following is not a cognitive disability.
(a) Child suffering from dyslexia
(b) Child having problem in solving mathematical calculations
(c) Child having low IQ (under 70)
(d) Child facing speech disorders.

Short Answer (SA) Type Questions

1. Suggest a few ways that one should follow while dealing with the people facing mobility impairment.

2. Explain any three disability etiquettes that one should follow while dealing with the people who are audibly challenged?

3. Explain any three symptoms of ASD and ODD.

4. Explain the occurence of ODD in adults. What are the symptoms

5. What do you understand by adaptive physical education?

Long Answer (LA) Type Questions

1. Explain how nuclear accidents, poor access to healthcare and genetic mutations may cause disability

2. Difference between cognitive and intellectual disability. Mentions the symtoms of both the disabilities

Answers

1. (a)   *2.* (a)   *3.* (b)   *4.* (c)

CHAPTER 03

Physiology and Injuries in Sports

In this Chapter...

- Physiological Factors Determining Components of Physical Fitness
- Effects of Exercise on Cardio Respiratory System
- Effect of Exercise on Muscular System
- Sports Injuries
- Causes, Prevention and Treatment
- First-aid

Physiology is very essential to understand how to attain physical fitness in order to enhance the performance in sports. It is the scientific study of human body and its systems.

The scientific principles of exercise in physiology, are applied through a range of physiological interventions or assessments, which facilitate the profiling and monitoring of specific parameters relevant to optimise sports performance.

In other words, it can be said that physiology is basically the study of how exercises or sports activities alter the structure and functioning of our body.

Physiological Factors Determining Components of Physical Fitness

The components of physical fitness are determined by the physiological factors. The main components of physical fitness are **strength**, **speed**, **endurance**, **flexibility**, etc. These components that make a person physically fit and their determining factors are described as follows

Muscular Strength

One of the basic requirements for success in all movements is muscular strength. It may be defined as the maximum force or tension a muscle or a muscle group can exert against a resistance.

Physiologically, the muscle will increase it's strength only through increasing intensity and duration of workout. This is called the principle of overload.

The development of strength is specific to the muscle or muscles involved in a particular activity.

Factors Determining Strength

The factors which determine strength are explained as follows

1. **Size of the Muscle** The size of the muscle determines the strength possessed by an individual. It is well-known fact that bigger and larger muscles can produce more force.

   Males have bigger and larger muscles due to which they have more strength than females.

   The muscle size can be increased with the help of various methods such as weight training, etc., which will also improve the muscular strength.

2. **Body Weight** There is a positive correlation between the body weight and strength. It has been noticed that individuals with heavier body weight are stronger than the individual with the lighter weight. Thus, body weight also determines the strength of an individual.

3. **Muscle Composition** Muscles consist of two types of fibres *i.e. fast twitch fibres* (white fibres) and *slow twitch fibres* (red fibres).

   The fast twitch fibres are capable to contract faster and therefore, they can produce more force.

   On the contrary, the slow twitch fibres are not capable to contract faster but they are capable to contract for a longer duration.

   Muscles containing more percentage of fast twitch fibres produce more strength. The percentage of fast and slow twitch fibres is genetically determined and cannot be changed through training.

4. **Nerve Impulse** The nervous system also plays an important role in muscle strength. A muscle consists of many motor units. The number of contracting motor units determines the total force. If muscles contract with greater intensity, more strength will be produced.

5. **Age** Age is a factor which effects the muscle strength. Muscle strength is maximum generally in the age of 15-30 years.

   It declines with the age but it is primarily due to decrease in muscle cross-sectional area and a decline in the number of contractile tissues within the muscle fibres. Regular strength training limits loss of muscle strength with ageing.

Speed

It is the rapidity with which one repeats successive movements in the same pattern. It may also be defined as the ability of a person to move quickly over a distance.

For example, 50 m and 100 m dashes. Individuals with greater speed usually also have superior reaction time.

Factors Determining Speed

Factors which determine the speed are explained as follows

1. **Bio-chemical Reserves and Metabolic Power** For maximum speed performance, the muscles require more amount of energy at a very high rate of consumption.

   For this purpose, the phosphogen Adenosine Triphosphate (ATP) and Creatine Phosphate (CP) storage in the muscles should be enough.

   If ATP and CP storage is less in contracting muscles, the muscle contractions due to insufficient energy supply become slow after a short time.

The metabolic power depends upon the energy supplied through certain enzymes. Proper working of the enzymes means high rate of metabolism which increases speed of doing work.

2. **Muscle Composition** Muscles consist of two types of fibres *i.e. fast twitch fibres (white fibres)* and *slow twitch fibres (red fibres)*. A person containing more of fast twitch fibres will have greater speed.

3. **Mobility of the Nervous System** The rapid contraction and relaxation of the muscles take place due to rapid excitation (state of enhanced activity of the cell) of the nervous system. The rapid movements give greater speed.

   The nervous system can maintain this rapid excitation and inhibition only for a few seconds after which the excitation spreads to the neighbouring centres causing tension in the entire body. This results in decrease in speed.

   The mobility of the nervous system can be trained only to a limited extent.

4. **Explosive Strength** very quick and explosive movements, explosive strength is indispensable. It depends upon metabolic composition, muscle size and muscle coordination.

   The explosive strength of the muscles can be improved through training, which will also improve the speed upto a certain limit.

5. **Flexibility** Flexibility refers to the range of movement around a joint. It covers all joints and has significant impact on performance.

   Lack of good flexibility can have a direct negative impact on speed due to the limitations of joint motion. Flexibility helps in enhancing speed by utilising explosive power.

Endurance

It can be defined as the ability of a muscle or muscle group to perform repeated contractions against a resistance / load or to sustain contraction for an extended period of time with less discomfort and more rapid recovery.

In other words, it is the ability to withstand fatigue.

Factors Determining Endurance

The factors which determine the endurance are explained as follows

Aerobic Capacity

It refers to the capacity to maintain the adequate supply of oxygen (O_2) to the working muscles. This influences the level of endurance.

If the muscles get adequate supply of O_2 for a longer duration, then the athlete will have more endurance.

The aerobic capacity is influenced by O_2 intake, O_2 transport, O_2 uptake and energy reserves. These are as follows

- **Oxygen Intake** It is the amount of O_2 taken by the lungs. This intake depends on the vital capacity, lung size, number of active alveoli, strength of respiratory muscles and size of chest cavity.
- **Oxygen Transport** The oxygen transport depends on the amount of oxygen, which the blood has absorbed from the lungs and the ability of the circulatory system to carry this quickly to the working muscles.
  The amount of oxygen absorbed into the blood depends on the speed of blood flow through the lungs and on the blood haemoglobin.
  The transportation of oxygenated blood depends on the capacity of heart. This capacity can be improved by training.
- **Oxygen Uptake** It is the amount of O_2 that can be absorbed and consumed by the working muscles from the blood.
  This depends on the blood flow, temperature, pressure of O_2 in the blood, metabolic capacity of mitochondria, speed and amount of O_2 consumption.
- **Energy Reserves** It means the availability of fuel to the muscles for getting energy. This depends on the muscle glycogen and sugar level in the blood.
  A person having high energy reserves will have high endurance capacity and *vice-versa*. If the energy reserves fall down upto a certain level, then fatigue occurs.

Anaerobic Capacity

The working capacity of muscle in absence of oxygen is called anaerobic capacity. More or less anaerobic capacity is required in all kinds of endurance activities.

Anaerobic capacity depends on the following factors

- **Phosphagen Store** It consists of Adrenosine Triphosphate (ATP) and Phosphocereatine (CP) which helps in producing energy.
- **Buffer Capacity** It means total storage of Alkali reserve in the body to fight against the effect of lactic acid.
- **Lactic Acid Tolerance** The ability to tolerate the higher concentration of lactic acid is a very important factor in determining anaerobic capacity. This is important for sports as high level of endurance is required. This tolerance capacity can be improved through training.

Movement Economy

Energy may be saved if the movements are correct, so the economical movements are necessary for enchancing endurance.

Economical movements varies from one sport or exercise to another. For example, in football, 15-25% of the energy can be saved, if the movements are correct.

Muscle Composition

Among the presence of fast and slow twitch fibres, the slow twitch fibres are useful for endurance. Therefore, muscle composition containing more of slow twitch fibres is good for endurance activities.

Flexibility

In general, flexibility is that quality of the muscles, ligaments and tendons that enables the joints of the body to move easily through a complete range of movement.

More flexibility of the joints give better movement of limbs, increased speed and enhances better control of the body.

Factors Determining Flexibility

The factors which determine the flexibility are discuss as follows

1. **Joint Structure** The joint structure of a person determines the range of motions and hence level the **flexibility** of an individual.
   For example, the ball and socket joint of the shoulder has the greatest range of motion in comparison to the knee joint.

2. **Age and Gender** The age of a person as well as the gender determines the level of flexibility. Flexibility decreases with the advancement of age. Females are more flexible than males. It can be enhanced with the help of training, as strength and endurance are enhanced.

3. **Stretchability of Muscles** If the muscles are regularly stretched, then they remain flexible. The stretchability of muscles depends on the amount of exercises and physical activities.

4. **Previous Injury** Any kind of internal or external injury may lead to thickening or shrinking of fibrous tissues which may become less elastic. This can lead to reduction in flexibility.

5. **Internal Environment** Internal environment of the athlete influences the flexibility. For example, 10 minutes of warm bath increases body temperature and flexibility whereas 10 minutes staying outside in 10°C reduces body temperature and flexibility.

6. **Muscle Strength** The muscle should have a minimum level of strength to make the movement, especially against the gravity or external force. Weak muscles can become a limitation for achieving higher range of movement.

   Muscle strength is highly trainable and therefore can enhance flexibility of a person to a great extent.

7. **Active and Sedentary Lifestyle** Regular activities enhance the flexibility, whereas inactive individual loses flexibility due to the soft tissues and joints shrinking and losing extensibility.

Effects of Exercise

Effect of exercise on Cardiorespiratory system and muscular respiratory system are as follows

Effects of Exercise on Cardiorespiratory System

The functioning and efficiency of cardiorespiratory system reduces with age. In order to keep it in perfect condition, exercises are pre-requisite.

Exercises helps in improving the functioning of cardiorespiratory system, which increases the overall fitness of an individual.

Frequent exercises helps in reducing risk of cardiorespiratory diseases. Exercises increases cardiac output, heart size, blood pressure, etc. thus they should be performed regularly.

Effects of exercise on cardiorespiratory system are

1. **Increase in Heart Size**

   Regular exercises develop the muscles of the heart. It increases the size of the heart along with the strengthening of heart.

   Thus, the heart becomes more efficient in doing its job with the capacity to pump more oxygen-rich blood.

2. **Decrease in Cholesterol Level**

   Regular exercise reduces the level of cholesterol in our blood. The level of cholesterol in our blood is directly linked with blood pressure.

   Exercise decreases the level of low-density protein and increases the level of high-density protein.

   It simply means that exercise decreases the LDL (bad cholesterol) and increases HDL (good cholesterol).

3. **Heart Rate**

   The number of cardiac contradictions per minute is called heart rate. If a 10-week training programme is allotted to an individual whose initial resting heart rate is 72 beats per minute, after the training, his resting heart rate may be reduced upto 10 beats per minute.

   Thus, a proper and long-term training programme decreases the resting heart rate.

4. **Stroke Volume**

   The volume of blood pumped into the heart with every heartbeat is known as the stroke volume. In an untrained male, it is 50-70 ml/beat. In a trained male athlete, it may be 70-90 ml/beat. The stroke volume increases in response to the intensity of the exercises and also pumps more blood when required.

5. **Blood Flow**

   Regular exercise increases blood flow in the body. During exercises, muscles need more blood, then body increases number of capillaries. The existing capillaries also open wider.

   With increasing intensities of exercise, a greater accumulation of lactic acid and the production of other metabolic end products (potassium, phosphate) occurs. This increases blood flow in the cardiac output, while it decreases in kidneys and abdomen.

6. **Cardiac Output**

   It is the amount of blood pumped by the heart in one minute. In other words, it is the product of stroke volume and heart rate. Cardiac output increases with the intensity of the exercises.

   The cardiac output in untrained individuals may be 14-20 l/min, in trained individuals 25-35 l/min and in the best athletes, the cardiac output can be upto 40 l/min at rest.

   It is calculated according to the following formula

   Cardiac Output = Heart Rate × Stroke Volume

7. **Quick Recovery**

   A healthy heart means quick recovery from the workout. The heart becomes normal quickly after vigorous exercises and also pumps more blood when required.

8. **Blood Pressure**

   During the exercise, systolic blood pressure (pressure against artery walls during heartbeats) can increase while diastolic blood pressure (pressure against artery wall while heart is resting) usually remains unchanged even during the intensive exercise.

9. **Decrease in Rate of Respiration**

   When a beginner starts exercise, then his rate of respiration increases. But when the same individual performs exercise on regular basis, then his rate of respiration at rest decreases in comparison to the beginning stage.

10. **Lung Volume**

    For normal breathing at rest, lung expand and there is a change in air pressure. During exercise, due to rapid movement of diaphragm and intercostal muscles, total area of lung expands to accommodate more exchange of gases.

11. **Tidal Volume**

    It is the amount of air inhaled by a person during a normal breath. It is around 500 ml per inhale for a healthy adult.

    During exercise, this tidal volume increases. Depending on the intensity it may be 1500-2000 ml for ordinary person and for well-trained athlete, it may be increased to 2500 ml.

12. **Lung Diffusion Capacity**

    During exercise, the lung diffusion capacity increases in both trained and untrained persons. However, trained athletes may increase their diffusion capacity 30% more than that of an untrained person because athlete's lung surface area and red blood cell count is higher than that of non-athletes.

13. **Pulmonary Ventilation**

    The amount of air passing through lungs each minute is called Pulmonary Ventilation (PV). The PV is a product of **Tidal Volume** (TV) and **Respiratory Rate** (RR) and therefore at rest it is around 8 l/min.

    During exercise time, both TV and RR increases, due to which PV will also increase depending on the intensity of exercise.

    For ordinary person, the value of PV may be 40-50 l/min and for well-trained athlete, it may be around 100 l/min.

14. **Oxygen Uptake**

    It is the amount of O_2 that can be absorbed by the working muscles from the blood. It is also called VO_2. The oxygen uptake increases due to exercises, thus providing the body with greater oxygen.

15. **Residual Air Volume**

    It is the volume of air in the lungs which is left after exhalation. With exercises, the residual air capacity increases which enhances efficiency of lungs.

16. **Vital Air Capacity**

    It is the sum of tidal volume, inspiratory reserve volume and expiratory reserve volume. It is the maximum amount of air a person can expel from the lungs after a maximum inhalation.

    This capacity rises with the increase in exercises and varies from 3500 cc to 4500 cc in a normal adult.

Effects of Exercise on Muscular System

Muscular system plays a very significant role in the functioning of body. Exercise works as a stimulus and gives stress to muscles. It improves both strength and endurance of muscular system of an individual.

It involves a series of sustained muscle contractions, of either long or short duration, depending upon the nature of physical activity.

Following are the effects of exercise on the muscular system

1. **Increase in Muscle Temperature**

   Muscles are very inefficient and much of the energy we use to contract them is lost as heat. However, the increase in muscle temperature (between one to two degrees) during an exercise enables your muscles to be more flexible.

2. **Muscle Size**

   Although muscle size (and other physical characteristics such as height) is largely determined by a person's genes but muscle size also gets affected by the intensity of exercises. For example, in weightlifting, the diameter of the muscles increases.

3. **Increase in Lactate Threshold**

   Exercise increases the ability of the muscles to tolerate lactic acid. This increases endurance as the working capacity of the muscles rises due to delayed tiredness and fatigue.

4. **Muscle Coordination**

   Frequent exercise and special use of specific muscles for the same or similar skilled tasks, like dribbling a ball in a game of football, leads to improved coordination.

5. **Muscle Biochemistry**

   Many beneficial biochemical changes take place in muscle tissues as a result of regular long-term exercises, such as increase in the size and quantity of mitochondria in the cells, increase in the activity of enzymes.

6. **Increase in Muscle Mass**

   Regular exercise and physical activities increase the muscle mass of a person, thus making him stronger, fitter and healthier.

7. **Increases Alertness**

   Physical activity or exercise, in the short-term, can increase your alertness as hormones are released. These hormones can also help you to feel more relaxed after the activity.

8. **Delays Fatigue**

   Regular exercise delays the onset of fatigue as exercise develops the fitness levels and increases endurance thereby delaying fatigue.

9. **Helps in Maintaining Toned Muscles**

   Regular exercise helps in keeping the muscles in toned position. Muscles become firm and maintain a slight and a steady pull on the attachments.

10. **Helps You Control Your Weight**

    Along with diet, exercise plays an important role in controlling your weight and preventing obesity.

    To maintain your weight, the calories you eat and drink must equal the energy you burn. To lose weight, you must use more calories than you intake.

Sports Injuries

A sports injury may be defined as "damage to the tissues of the body that occurs as a result of sport or exercise". They are commonly caused by overuse, direct impact, or the application of force that is greater than the force that a body part can structurally withstand.

There are two kinds of sports injuries *i.e. acute* and *chronic*. **Acute injury** is a injury that occurs suddenly, such as sprained ankle caused by an awkward landing while, **chronic injury** is caused by repeated overuse of muscle groups or joints.

Poor technique and structural abnormalities can also contribute to the development of chronic injuries.

Medical investigation of any sports injury is important, because the person may be hurt more severely than he/she thinks.

Classification of Sports Injuries

Sports injuries can be classified according to the type of tissues. They are

Soft Tissue Injuries

This type of injury includes damage of muscles, sprain, strain, abrasion, laceration etc. in which injury is caused on soft tissue of the skin, muscles, tendons, synovial membrane, fibrous tissue, fat, blood vessels, nerves and ligaments in body.

For example, a sprained ankle. Soft tissue injuries occur more than hard tissue injuries. These are explained as below

1. Abrasion

It is a shallow wound, typically a wearing away of the top layer of skin (the epidermis) due to an applied friction force against the body. It may be caused by falling on a hard surface.

The scraped-off surface layer of skin from an abrasion can contain particles of dust or dirt, which may lead to an infection or other complications, if not cleaned and attended properly.

Abrasions are distinguished from **incised wounds**, which are much more serious injuries. While an abrasion is an injury that damages only the superficial layers of skin, incised wound is a deeper cut (typically with a sharp object), that has the potential for serious and severe bleeding.

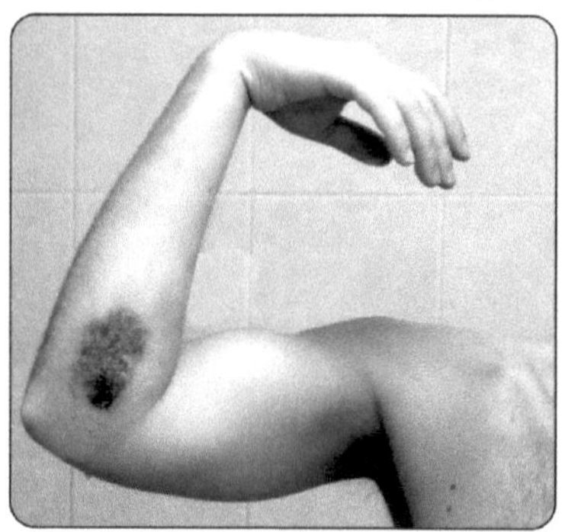
Abrasion

Prevention

It is difficult to fully prevent an abrasion, as it is often accidental. Some of the precautionary steps are

- Wear gloves, long sleeves, pants or other layers of clothing as additional layers of protection for the skin.
- Sports equipment should be of good quality.
- Wear helmets and protective pads for knees, wrists, elbows and hands during sports.
- Wear safety gears such as safety goggles, closed-toe shoes and glasses.
- Keep a well-stocked first-aid kit which can help in immediate treatment for abrasions, and can help lessen the severity of injuries as they are encountered.
- Learn the correct techniques before taking part in sports.
- Players should remain alert during play and follow rules and regulations of the game.

2. Contusion

Contusion is a **muscle injury**. It can be caused by a direct hit with any sports equipments. It generally happens when an injured capillary or blood vessel leaks blood into the surrounding area.

The raised area of contusion is due to the accumulation of blood and fluid from the injured blood vessels in the tissue. Stiffness and swelling are common features of contusion.

Soft tissue contusions are much easier to diagnose than bone contusions because they have distinct characteristics like

- discoloured skin that looks red, green, purple, blue or black.

- a small bump over the area in some cases.
- pain that is usually worse when pressure is applied to the area.

While both muscle and skin tissue contusions cause pain, muscle tissue contusions are usually more painful, especially if they affect a muscle that you can't avoid using.

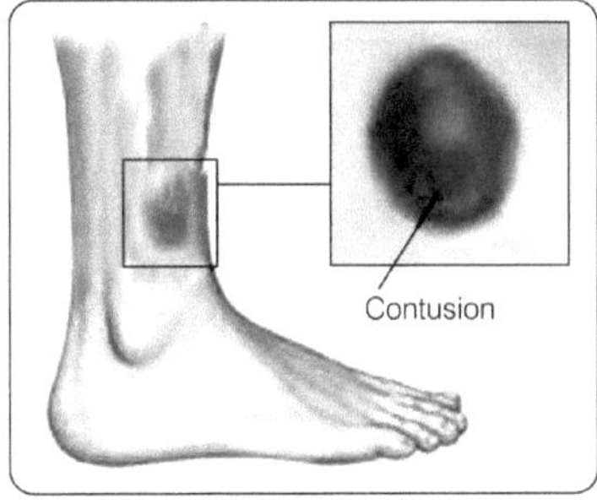

Contusion

Prevention

- Carry a flashlight when walking through poorly lit areas to reduce the risk of accidental falls.
- Play fields/courts should be clear of obstructions as well as it should be smooth and clean.
- Wear helmets or other protective equipment when playing contact sports, such as soccer.
- Sports equipments of good quality should be used in games and sports.
- Players should be careful and alert during the practice and competition.
- Proper warm-up is essential to prevent an injury and stretch all the muscles involved in the upcoming exercise, activity or practice.

3. Laceration

It is basically **tearing of the skin** that results in an irregular wound. Lacerations may be caused by injury with a sharp object or by impact injury from a blunt object or force. They may occur anywhere on the body.

In most cases, tissue injury is minimal, and infections are uncommon. Severe lacerations are often accompanied by significant bleeding and pain.

Cleaning and preparing a laceration for repair is crucial for preventing infection and reducing the appearance of scarring.

Prevention

- Lacerations are best prevented by maintaining proper equipment and by enforcing safety rules.
- After the injury, wound care should be carried out to prevent possible complications of infection and scarring. This includes keeping the wound clean and dry.

- Keeping the muscles warm will prevent acute injuries and will stave off overuse injuries by allowing the body to prepare steadily and safely. So, warm-up helps to prevent injury during exercise.
- Proper cooling down is also instrumental in the prevention of injury as warm-up.

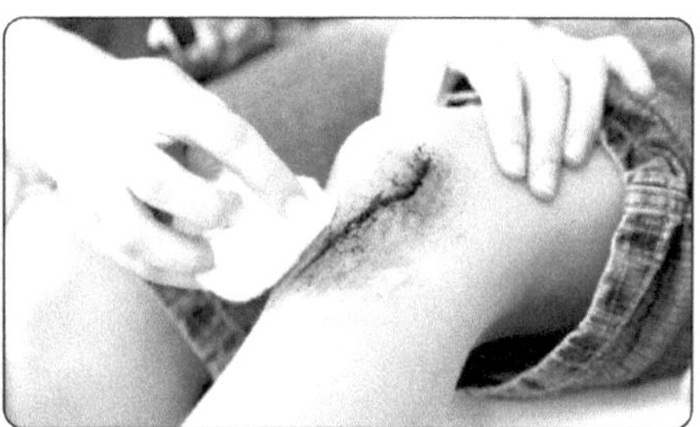

Laceration

4. Incision

An incision wound is a **cut in the skin** caused by a sharp object such as a knife, broken glass, scissors, etc. However, occasionally these types of wounds can be very deep, cutting into muscle tissue, tendons or major blood vessels. Damage to major blood vessels can cause life-threatening bleeding.

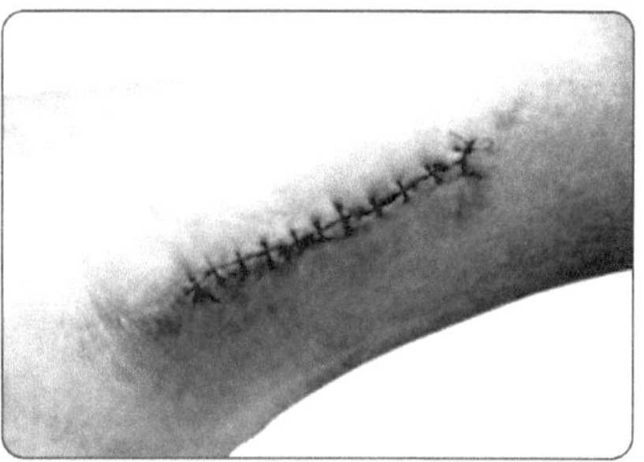

Incision

Examples of incised wounds include

- Surgical incisions.
- Cuts to the skin due to accident.
- Cutting of your skin due to broken glass.

Prevention

- Incisions are best prevented by maintaining proper equipment and by enforcing safety rules.
- Athletes or players should warm-up before each exercise or sports session and cool down afterwards.
- They should stretch regularly, use good technique and be mindful of fatigue and dehydration which can impair concentration and lead to an injury.
- After the injury, wound care should be carried out to prevent possible complications of infection.

5. Strain

A strain is defined as an **injury to a tendon** (tissues that connect your muscles and bones) or **muscle**. Strains often occur in the lower back and the muscle in the back of the thigh.

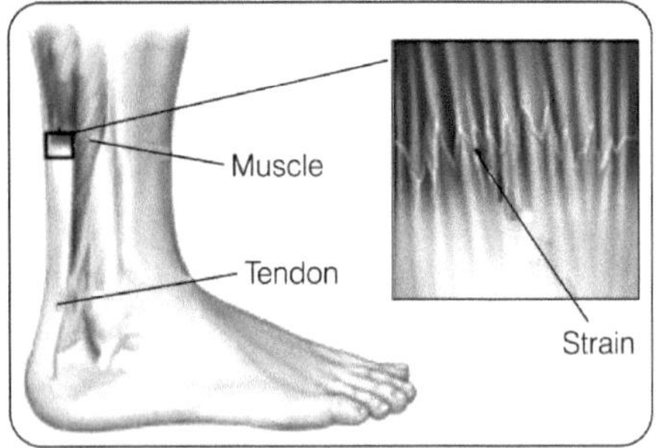

Strain

Some of the symptoms include pain, swelling, muscle spasms and limited ability to move the muscle.

Contact sports like soccer, football, hockey, boxing and wrestling put people at risk for strains. Strain can happen as sudden (acute) strain or develop over days (chronic).

An **acute strain** is caused by trauma or an injury such as a blow to the body. It can also be caused by improperly lifting heavy objects or over-stressing the muscles.

Chronic strains are usually the result of overuse prolonged, repetitive movements of muscles and tendons.

Prevention

- Warm-up to prepare for exercise, even after stretching. Warming up increases your heart and blood flow rates and loosens up muscles, tendons, ligaments and joints.
- Sports equipments must be of good quality.
- Develop a balanced fitness program that incorporates cardiovascular exercise, strength training and flexibility. Add activities and new exercises cautiously.
- Schedule regular days off from vigorous exercise and rest when tired.

6. Sprain

A sprain is a stretch or **tear of a ligament**, a strong band of connective tissue that connects the end of one bone with another. Ligaments stabilise and support the body's joints.

For example, ligaments in a knee connect your thigh bone (Femur) with your Shinbone (Tibia), enabling you to walk.

The areas of the body that are most vulnerable to sprain are the ankles, knees and wrists.

A sprained ankle can occur when your foot turns inward, placing extreme tension on the ligaments of your outer ankle.

A sprained knee can result from a sudden twist, and a wrist sprain can occur if you fall onto an out stretched hand.

Sometimes, fracture is also possible along with the sprain. In such injury, pain, bruising, swelling and inflammation are common symptoms.

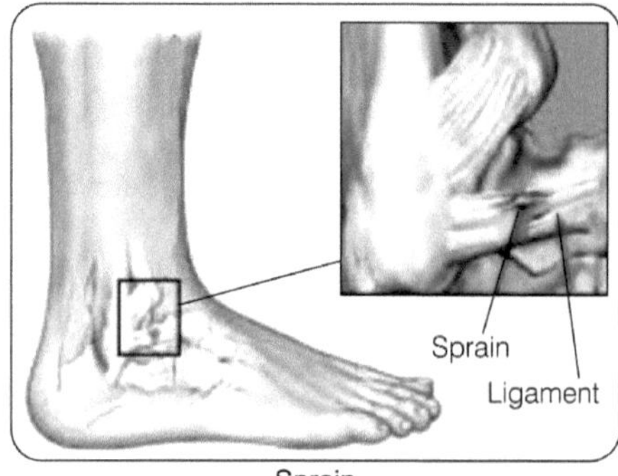

Sprain

Prevention

- Warm-up to prepare for exercise, even after stretching. Warming up increases your heart and blood flow rates and loosens up muscles, tendons, ligaments and joints.
- All the sports equipment must be of good quality.
- Develop a balanced fitness program that incorporates cardiovascular exercise, strength training and flexibility. Add activities and new exercises cautiously.
- Maintain a healthy weight and try to eat a well balanced diet to keep your muscles strong.
- Wear comfortable, loose-fitting clothes that let you move freely and are light enough to release body heat.

Hard Tissue Injuries/Bone and Joint Injuries

The hard tissue injuries take place in bones and cartilages, e.g. a fracture. These injuries are also known as bone and joint injuries.

The nature of the damage depends on the direction of the applied force on the bones and the manner in which these bones are attached to other structures.

This type of injuries are explained below

Bone Injury: Fracture

A hard tissue injury is also called a 'fracture' and is defined as a "loss of continuity in the substance of a bone".

In other words, it is a bone injury that breaks the continuity. of bone or seperate it into two or more parts.

Fracture is of various types, which are as follows

1. Stress Fracture

A stress fracture is an overuse injury. It occurs when muscles become fatigued and are unable to absorb added shock.

Eventually, the fatigued muscle transfers the overload of stress to the bone causing a tiny crack, called a stress fracture.

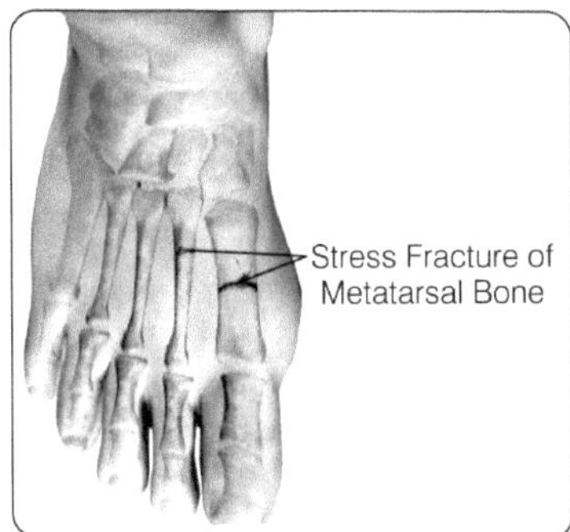

Stress Fracture

It is often the result of increasing the amount or intensity of an activity too rapidly.

It can also be caused by the impact of an unfamiliar surface (like, a tennis player who has switched surfaces from a soft clay court to a hard court), improper equipment (like, a runner wearing less flexible shoes) and increased physical stress (like, a basketball player who has had a substantial increase in playing time).

Most stress fractures occur in the weight-bearing bones of the lower leg and the foot.

2. Greenstick Fracture

A greenstick fracture occurs when a **bone bends** and **cracks**, instead of breaking completely into separate pieces.

Most greenstick fractures occur in children younger than 10 years of age because their bones are softer and more flexible than the bones of adults.

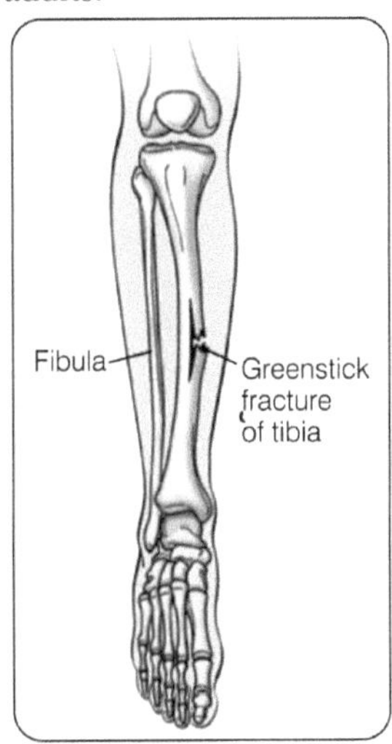

Greenstick Fracture

In this type of fracture, arm fractures are most common than leg fractures. It can be caused by many things like participation in sports, motor vehicle accidents and falls.

3. Comminuted Fracture

It is a **break or splinter of the bone** into more than two fragments. Since considerable force and energy is required to fragment bone, fractures of this kind occurs after high-impact trauma such as vehicular accidents.

This type of fracture is usually challenging to treat because the break is so complex.

4. Oblique Fracture

An oblique fracture is characterised by a break that is **curved** or at a **diagonal angle to the bone**. A sharp blow that comes from an angle (i.e. above or below) may cause oblique fractures.

They are particularly prone to angulation in the plane of the fracture. Trauma, sudden twist of the muscles or bone diseases may cause oblique fracture.

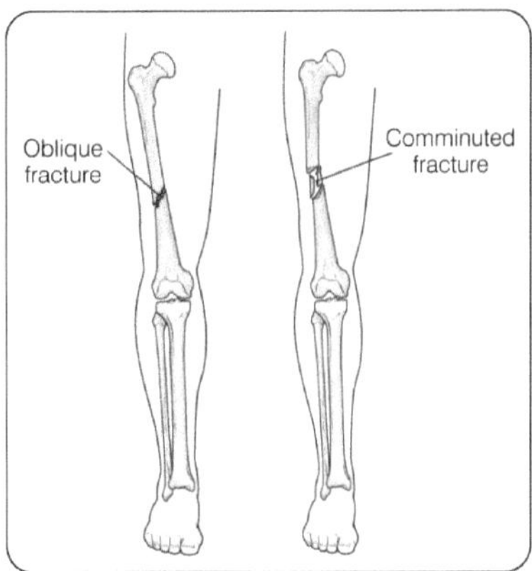

Oblique Fracture　　　Comminuted Fracture

5. Transverse Fracture

It is a fracture where the **bone breaks at a right angle** to the long axis of the bone.

Transverse fractures most often occur as the result of strong force applied perpendicular to the long axis of a bone.

This may also be caused due to trauma, sudden twisting of the bone due to muscle spasm or indirect loss of leverage or by certain bone diseases.

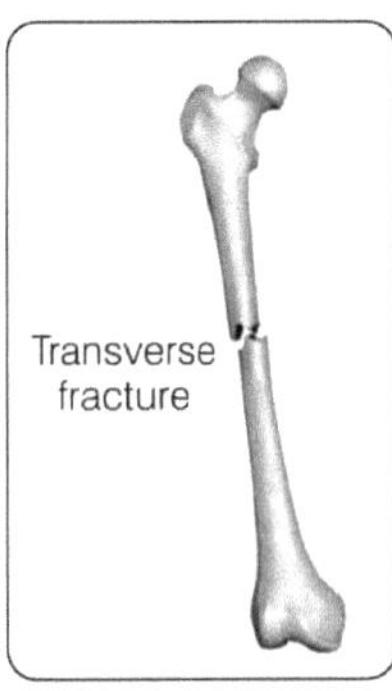

Transverse Fracture

6. Impacted Fracture

An impacted fracture is one whose ends of cracked bones are driven into each other. This commonly occurs with arm fractures in children and is sometimes known as a buckle fracture.

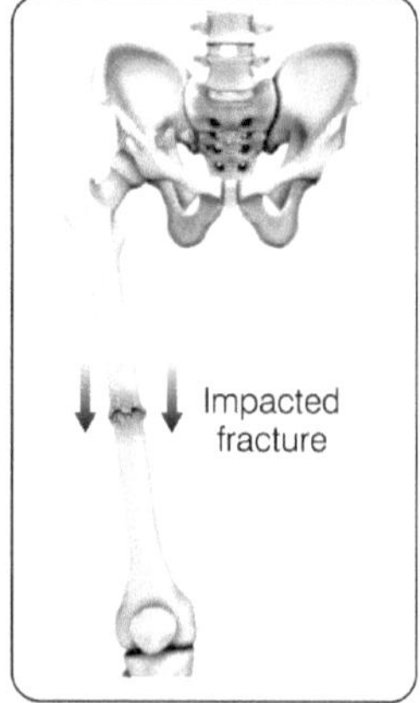
Impacted Fracture

In other words, it is a fracture caused when bone fragments are driven into each other. Lifting overweight item is one of the main causing factors of this fracture.

Prevention

- Having a healthy diet, exercising regularly and sticking to the recommended calcium intake will generally reduce the chances of suffering from a fracture. This will help to build strong bones and keep the body fit and healthy.
- Conditioning exercises during practice help to strengthen muscles.
- Rest periods during practice and games can reduce injuries.
- Players should be very careful and alert during practice, training and competition.

Joint Injuries

Joint injuries typically occur in the knees, ankles, wrists, shoulders and elbows. They can range from sprains to fractures and dislocations.

A **dislocation** is a separation of two bones where they meet at a joint. A dislocated joint is a joint where the bones are no longer in their normal positions.

A dislocated joint may be accompanied by numbness or tingling at the joint or beyond it. It is intensely painful, especially if you try to use joint or put weight on it.

Some of the common joint dislocations are

1. Shoulder Dislocation

This occurs when the ball of the upper arm bone (humerus) pops out of the shoulder socket. It is usually caused by a fall on to the upper arm or during contact sports such as Rugby.

Usually, the dislocated ball pops out at the front of the shoulder joint, where the supporting muscles are at their weakest.

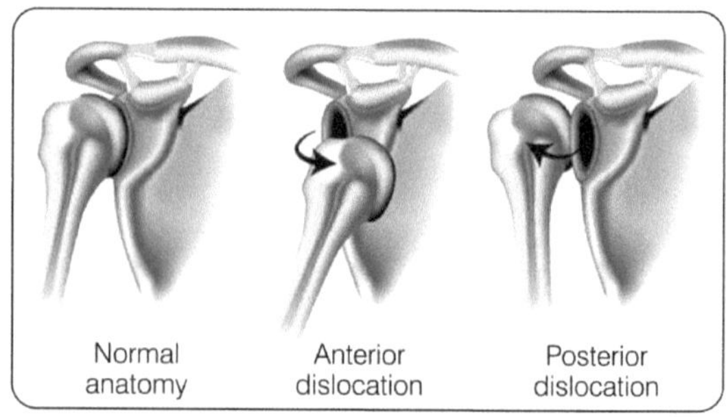

Shoulder Dislocation

2. Elbow Dislocation

The elbow is the second most common dislocation in adults. It takes a lot of force to dislocate the elbow, which is often an associated break in one of the bones. Dislocated elbows are at high risk of trapping blood vessels and need urgent attention.

The most common cause is falling and landing on your outstretched hand or arm, pushing the forearm bone sideways out of the joint.

Sports like cycling, gymnastics, etc. tend to be the most common sports causing elbow dislocation.

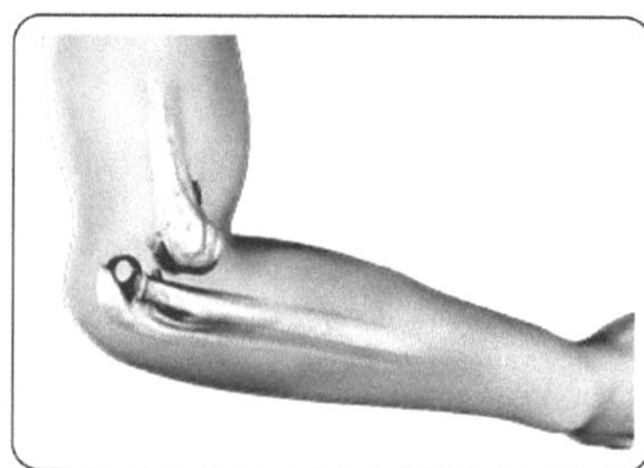
Elbow Dislocation

3. Dislocated Finger

This is a common injury which can affect any finger joint but most commonly affects the middle knuckle of the four fingers (rather than the thumb).

It is usually caused either by over-bending the finger backwards or catching the finger somewhere during fast movement.

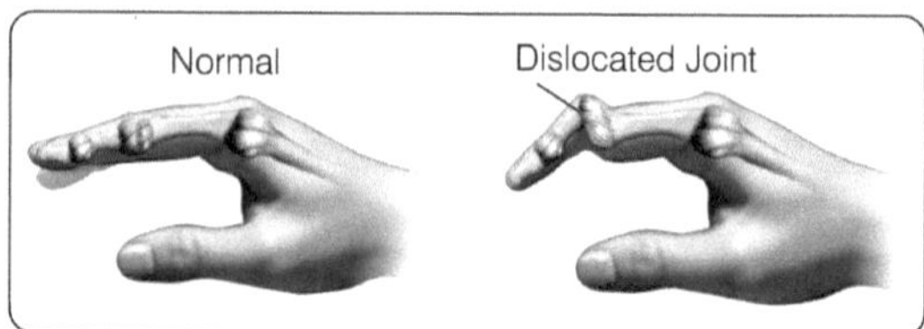

Dislocated Finger

This happens during sports activities when player try to stop the fast balls with the hand.

4. Wrist Dislocation

Wrist dislocation means dislocation of any of the eight small bones which make up the wrist. It is usually caused by a fall on the wrist or the outstretched arm. Symptoms include pain and obvious distortion of the wrist.

5. Ankle Dislocation

Dislocation of ankle joint is a rare injury but can happen in sports.

It is more common when there is an ankle fracture at the same time, as that can make the ankle joint unstable.

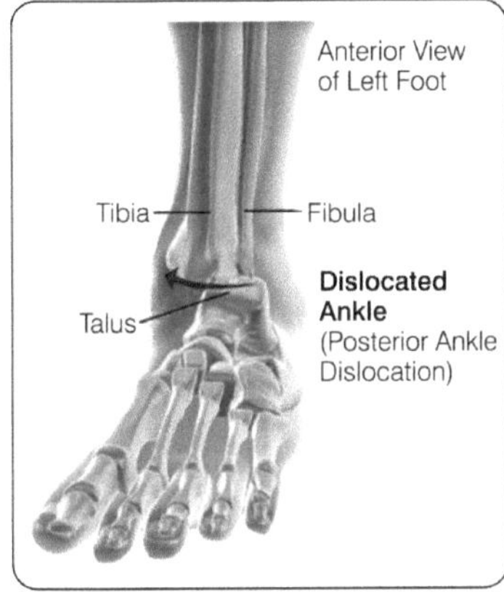

Ankle Dislocation

Prevention

- Improved strengthening of muscles around joints through fitness training, healthy diet and appropriate weight.
- Minimisation of risk taken during sports activities by using appropriate equipment and specific training or technique.
- Seeking medical advice if dislocation becomes repeated (recurrent). There may be a preventative operation which would stop the dislocations.
- In the case of recurrent dislocations, avoid the activities and positions which tend to cause it.
- Improved balance through fitness and exercises which strengthen the body's core muscles.
- Avoid falls as far as possible and perform regular exercise around your shoulder, wirst joints, etc.

Causes of Sports Injuries

To be able to effectively diagnose, rehabilitate and ultimately prevent subsequent injury, it is essential to understand the causes of sports injuries.

Some common causes of sports injury are

1. **Anatomical Factors** These are related to the anatomy of the body. Differences in leg length and body misalignment can lead to unequal forces being transferred to the tissues. This can cause injuries to ankle, hip and back.

2. **Individual Factors** These are specific to each individual and their medical history. Previous injuries and conditions can make a person more at risk of injury.

3. **Overtraining** Training too often, training at high intensity or having inadequate recovery time between trainings can cause overtraining, which in turn results to sports injuries.

   The common symptoms of overtraining are excessive fatigue, insomnia, impaired focus, inability to preform exercises, etc.

4. **Improper Warm-up** Improper warm-up often causes muscular cramps and strains as the body is not geared up to do exercises. Therefore, regular warm-up is necessary.

5. **Nutritional Inadequacy** Due to lack of nutrients in food can also be the reason or cause of sports injuries among the players. Deficiency of vitamin D, calcium, and phosphorous can lead to bone fracture.

6. **Equipment Selection Factors** These are related to the suitability of equipment. For example, an incorrect footwear will not protect the foot and ankle adequately. It will also not distribute forces effectively. Thus, it increases the risk of injury.

7. **Impact and Contact Causes** Several sports players pick up injuries that are caused by impact or contact with objects, surfaces or other people.

   These injuries are common in contact sports like football or rugby or in more dangerous sports like motor racing, boxing and skiing.

8. **Lack of Fitness** Fitness does not mean only physical fitness but it also includes the physiological and psychological fitness. Player who lacks in physiological or psychological fitness may get injured easily.

9. **Lack of Sports Facilities** Lack of sports facilities are also responsible for sport injuries upto a large extent.

   For instance, players playing in field, which is not smooth and there are many ditches in it, are at greater risk of getting injuries. Hence, proper sport facilities are prerequisite for preventing sport injures.

Prevention of Sports Injuries

In sports, a player is highly vulnerable to different type of injuries. Therefore, prevention of sport injuries is given topmost priority.

It includes two types of preventive measures *viz.* primary and secondary preventive measures. Primary preventive measures aim to reduce the occurrence of any injury in a sport.

Secondary preventive measures relate to the sports therapist examining the injured athlete to work out on how to reduce the risk of subsequent or secondary injuries.

General preventive measures that can prevent sports injuries are

1. **Warm-up and Cool-down** A well-structured warm-up and cool-down is necessary to either prepare the individual physically and mentally or aid recovery from sport/exercise.

   A good warm-up increases blood and nutrient flow to the muscles and increases concentration, which helps in avoiding injuries.

   Also, a good cool-down improves relaxation, flexibility and recovery of muscles.

2. **Using Protective Equipment** The use of protective equipment varies across different sports and exercises. The general purpose of protective equipment is to prevent harmful movements, reduce or disperse shock and force, and act as a shield to block force.

   Key pieces of protective equipment are footwear, helmet, goggles, gum shield, shin pads, gloves etc.

3. **Adherence to the Rules** If all performers are aware of and adhere to the rules and laws of the game, then injuries can be reduced.

4. **Regular Fitness Testing** Individuals must be fit enough to train or compete, otherwise their tissues can fail. Regular fitness testing will ensure individuals have the basic fitness to participate safely and effectively.

5. **Meeting Nutritional Requirements** Active individuals have increased nutritional requirements to meet extra energy, hydration and recover needs.

   Increasing carbohydrate, fluid and protein intake can play an important role in injury prevention by delaying fatigue and promoting recovery.

6. **Avoid Overtraining** Overtraining should be avoided by beginner, as it is one of the essential factors of causing injuries. Overtraining causes fatigue and also reduces concenteration.

   It also puts more pressure on muscles and bones. The training load should always be increased gradually and wisely.

7. **Proper Sports Facilities** There is a direct relationship between sports facilities and sports injuries. Proper and high standard sport facilities are prerequisite for the prevention of sport injuries.

   If playgrounds are maintained properly, the chances of getting injured on the playground will be reduced.

Treatment of Sports Injuries

Treatment of soft tissue injuries, bones and joint injuries is as follows

Treatment of Abrasion

- Clean the affected part with freshwater and do not aggressively scrub the wound. Gently remove dirt or any other particle present at the spot.

- Apply the medical ointment so that proliferation of bacteria does not take place.

- Use a clean bandage or piece of gauze with tape. This will prevent bacteria from infecting the area.

- Visit a doctor for proper dressing and tetanus injection, which is required to prevent the wound from causing an infection.

- Change the bandage or dressing as per instructions of the doctor.

Treatment of Contusion

- Firstly, apply cold compress to the area to reduce swelling. Ice or cold water should not be used for more than 40 minutes persistently. It should be performed several times a day.

- If there is more swelling at the area of contusion, then anti-inflammatory medicine can also be given.

- If there is no improvement in pain or swelling, then consult a doctor immediately.

- For rehabilitation, flexibility exercises should be performed carefully.

Treatment of Laceration

- Stop the flow of blood by applying firm pressure to the laceration with a clean cloth or gauze.

- Once bleeding has stopped, wash the wound with warm water and mild soap. Remove all dirt and debris carefully.

- For simple lacerations not requiring stitches, apply antibiotic ointment, and cover the wound area with a bandage and first-aid tape.

- Repeat the above step for fext new days, until wound gets healed. Also, continuously watch that there is no infection.

- If feel enormous pain during treatment procedure, then, take painkiller.

Treatment of Incision

- Treatment of incision depends on the location of the injury.
- Clean the wound properly with iodine tincture or spirit.
- If the wound is not deep, then first of all, place a piece of cotton with ointment and a bandage should be applied.
- Protect it from dirt and other particles.
- If the wound is too deep, then immediately visit a doctor and meanwhile apply cloth or bandage to prevent excessive bleeding.

Treatment of Sprain and Strain

PRICE Therapy

Minor injuries, such as mild sprains and strains, can often be initially treated at home using PRICE therapy for two or three days.

PRICE stands for Protection, Rest, Ice, Compression and Elevation. These are as follows

- **Protection** Protect the affected area from further injury by using a support.
- **Rest** Rest is essential to allow the wound to heal. Avoid exercise and reduce your daily physical activity. Using crutches or a walking stick may help if you can't put weight on your ankle or knee. A sling may help if you've injured your shoulder.
- **Ice** Apply an ice pack to the affected area for 15 to 20 minutes every two to three hours. A bag of frozen peas, or similar, will work well. Wrap the ice pack in a towel so that it doesn't directly touch your skin and cause an ice burn.
- **Compression** Use elastic compression bandages during the day to limit swelling as well as bleeding. A firm pad can be applied over a injured part with a strap around it to hold it in place. It should be applied very smoothly as it may hinder blood circulation.
- **Elevation** Keep the injured body part raised above the level of your heart whenever possible. This may also help to reduce swelling.

R.I.C.E. Therapy

RICE stands for Rest, Ice, Compression and Elevation. These are as follows

- **Rest the Injured Limb** Your doctor may recommend not putting any weight on the injured area for 48 to 72 hours, so you may need to use crutches. A splint or brace also may be helpful initially. But don't avoid all activity.

  Even with an ankle sprain, you can usually still exercise other muscles to minimise deconditioning.
- **Ice the Area** Use a cold pack, a slush bath or a compression sleeve filled with cold water to help limit swelling after an injury.

  Try to ice the area as soon as possible after the injury and continue to ice it for 15 to 20 minutes, four to eight times a day, for the first 48 hours or until swelling improves.

  If you use ice, be careful not to use it too long, as this could cause tissue damage.
- **Compression** Compress the area with an elastic wrap or bandage. Compressive wraps or sleeves made from elastic or neoprene are best.
- **Elevation** Elevate the injured limb above your heart whenever possible to help prevent or limit swelling.

  Sprains can take days to months to recover. As the pain and swelling improve, gently begin using the injured area.

Treatment of Stress Fracture

- To reduce swelling and relieve pain, apply ice packs to the affected area for 24 to 48 hours.
- It's important to give the bone times to heal. This may take several days or months. If pain persist, then take some painkillers.
- Avoid bearing weight and unnecessary movements.
- When swelling is reduced, start putting partial weight on the affected area. After two weeks, start putting normal weight.
- For a period of 6 to 8 weeks, avoid the activity that caused stress facture. Then, start doing activity slowly.

Treatment of Greenstick Fracture

- In most cases, these fractures are treated by immobilising the bone with a splint. This splint remain in place for 4 to 6 weeks.
- The swelling that occurred on the site of the fracture may be reduced with anti-inflammatory drugs.
- Pain can be relieved by taking pain relievers.
- Normally, it takes 8 weeks for compelete bone healing.
- High impact activities should be avoided in the beginning.

Treatment of Comminuted Fracture

- Someone with a comminuted fracture will probably need surgery. Then, he or she will need to wear a splint or cast for a while to keep the bone from moving while it heals.
- For pain management, painkillers should be given to the affected person.
- Antibiotics should be given to avoid infections.
- It may take for more than few months to restore to its normal condition. After that, physical therapy should be used to treat completely.

Treatment of Oblique Bone Fracture

- The treatment method of oblique bone fracture usually depends upon the amount of damage to the bone.
- In most of the oblique fractures, surgical treatment is required.
- If the damage is extensive, metal rods and screws are used to hold the bone in place.
- If the damage to the bone is minimum then, a plaster cast may be used to treat the fracture.

Treatment of Transverse Fracture

- If the transverse injury is limited with no other injury, then it can be treated at home, hospital care is not necessary.
- During the first 2 days after injury, apply an ice pack to the painful area for 20 minutes in every 2 to 4 hours. This will help reduce swelling and pain. Don't put the ice pack directly on your skin. Wrap it in a towel before applying.

- Surgery is needed in case of multiple fractures of backbone, as there can be damage to spinal cord.
- This injury will take 4 to 6 weeks to heal. A back brace (called TSLO) or abdominal binder may be prescribed to reduce pain by limiting motion at the fracture site.
- After the healing time, you will be advised to gradually return to normal activities over the next 3 or 4 weeks.

Treatment of Impacted Fracture

- If an impacted fracture only involves a few bone fragments and the damage is not too significant or severe, immobilisation may be enough to treat it.
- The movement of the affected part should be minimised for quite some time even after a splint is removed.
- These fractures takes more time to heal. However, in severe cases, surgery is required to treat this fracture.

Treatment of Dislocation

- First of all, doctor will manipulate or reposition the joint back into place. Patient will be given a sedative or anaesthetic to remain comfortable and also to allow the muscles near joint to relax, which eases the procedure.
- After the joint returns to its proper place, doctor may ask the patient to wear a sling, splint, or cast for several weeks. This will prevent the joint from moving and allow the area to fully heal.
  The length of time that a joint needs to be immobile will vary, depending on the joint and severity of the injury.
- Most of the pain should go away after the joint returns to its proper place. However, the doctor may prescribe a pain reliever or a muscle relaxant if patient still feels pain.
- Rehabilitation begins after the doctor properly repositions or manipulates the joint into the correct position and removes the sling or splint.
  The goal of rehabilitation is to gradually increase the joint's strength and restore its range of motion.

First-aid

First-aid is the assistance given to any person suffering from a sudden illness or injury, with care provided to preserve life, prevent the condition from worsening, and/or promote recovery. It is normally performed until the next level of care, such as a paramedic or doctor arrives at the scene.

In other words, "it is an immediate and temporary care given to a victim of an accident or sudden illness before the services of a physician is obtained".

First-aid includes both self-help and home-care. This assistance is very useful and often determines the sequence of treatments to be followed after the initial first aid.

A person does not need a lot of equipments to give first aid. A package of a few materials such as antiseptic, bandage, scissors, cotton, plasters, wipes can be packed and first-aid kit is ready.

Aims and Objectives of First-aid

The aims and objectives of first aid are as follows

1. **Preserve Life** Main aim of first aid is to preserve life by carrying out emergency first aid procedures.

   Preserving life should always be the overall aim of all first aiders. This includes first aider's own life. We should never put ourselves or others in danger.

2. **Provide Relief from Pain and Suffering** The immediate objective of first-aid is to provide relief to wounded person from pain and suffering. Pain is natural in any type of accident and becomes unbearable in case of fracture or dislocation of joint during accident.

3. **Prevent Deterioration** The other important aim of first-aid is to prevent the casualty's condition from deteriorating any further.

   In addition, this aim includes preventing further injuries. We should attempt to make the area as safe as possible by removing any danger. If moving is not possible, we should attempt to remove the patient from the danger zone or call for specialist help.

4. **Promote Recovery** Finally, we can promote recovery by arranging prompt emergency medical help. In addition, simple first aid can significantly affect the long-term recovery of injury.

Chapter Practice

PART 1

Objective Questions

• Multiple Choice Questions

1. The capacity of muscles to absorb and consume oxygen is called
(a) Oxygen intake   (b) Oxygen uptake
(c) Oxygen gain   (d) Oxygen transfer

Ans. (b) The capacity of muscles to absorb and consume oxygen is called Oxygen uptake. It is the amount of O_2 that can be absorbed by the working muscles from the blood. It increases due to exercises.

2. Which factor of a person determines the range of motions and level of flexibility?
(a) Joint structure   (b) Internal environment
(c) Age and gender   (d) Previous injury

Ans. (a) Joint structure determines the range of motions and level of flexibility. If the joints are healthy and person is fit, then range of movements are possible.

3. The components of physical fitness are determined by the physiological factors. The main components of physical fitness are strength, speed, endurance, flexibility, etc. These components make a person physically fit.

Age and gender play a very important role in which of these components?
(a) Endurance   (b) Strength
(c) Explosive Strength   (d) Speed

Ans. (b) Age and gender play an important role in strength as strength is maximum from 15-30 years and males have muscles that produce greater force.

4. Early morning, we observe many older people following fitness regime. One day Ramu observed a 60-year-old man was holding his chest on the ground. When Ramu approached him, he said that he felt chest pain regularly after jogging.

What is the rate of normal heart beat of an adult?
(a) 72   (b) 80   (c) 65   (d) 90

Ans. (a) The rate of normal heart beat of an adult is 72 beats per minute. When some exercises or heavy work is done then the heart beat increases and slows down when a person is at rest or sleeping.

5. Identify the bone fracture shown in the image.

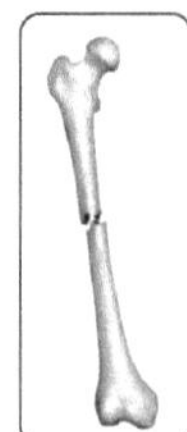

(a) Green Stick fracture   (b) Transverse fracture
(c) Comminuted fracture   (d) Stress fracture

Ans. (b) In the given image, the bone is broken at right angle on the long axis of the bone. This is called a transverse fracture.

6. Name the soft tissue injury shown below

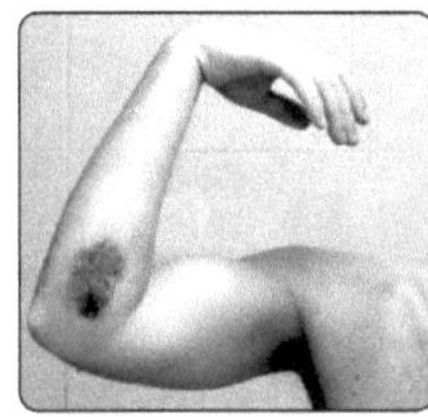

(a) Abrasion   (b) Contusion
(c) Laceration   (d) Incision

Ans. (a) The soft tissue injury shown in the image is abrasion.

7. Laceration is a ______.
(a) irregular cut on skin   (b) tissue injury
(c) seelling   (d) ligament injury

Ans. (a) Laceration is a irregular cut on the skin. It is mostly caused by impact injury from a blunt object or force.

8. Sprain is an injury of the ______.
(a) Muscle   (b) Ligament   (c) Joint   (d) Bone

Ans. (b) Sprain is an injury of the ligament. Ligaments are strong bands of connective tissue that connects the end of a bone with another.

9. The First-aid given to sprain injury are _____.
(a) RICE
(b) Following doctor's advice
(c) Giving massage to affected part
(d) Applying muscle ointment

Ans. (a) The First-aid given to sprain injury are RICE.

10. It is the fracture which occurs when a bone bends and cracks, instead of breaking completely into separate pieces.
(a) Transverse   (b) Comminuted
(c) Green Stick   (d) Stress

Ans. (c) Green Stick is a fracture which occurs when a bone bends and cracks, instead of breaking completely into separate pieces.

11. The Godavari School attended a CBSE Cluster Basketball Tournament. During the semi-final match Varun, one of the players fell down and was injured on the shoulder. He was immediately given first-aid by the coach Mr. Rahul, who had the knowledge of first-aid. Warm up session is essential for players to avoid any serious injuries during the match.
Example: Dislocation and fracture, sprain and strain.

Breakage of bones is called _____.
(a) Fracture   (b) Sprain
(c) Contusion   (d) Laceration

Ans. (a) The breakage of bones is called fracture which is defined as a hard tissue injury. Fractures take place at the bones and joints.

12. Sports instructor showed the students of class XII, how to give first-aid in case of minor injuries of sprain and strain. He told them about PRICE.

The letter 'C' in PRICE stands
(a) Conduction   (b) Compression
(c) Concussion   (d) Contraction

Ans. (b) PRICE is a therapy for treatment of sprain and strain. The letter 'C' in PRICE stands for compression.

13. Match the following.

List I (Components)		List II (Factors)
A.	Strength	1. Aerobic Capacity
B.	Speed	2. Muscle Size
C.	Flexibility	3. Explosive Strength
D.	Endurance	4. Stretchability of Muscles

Codes

	A	B	C	D			A	B	C	D
(a)	2	3	4	1		(b)	1	2	3	4
(c)	4	2	1	3		(d)	3	1	2	4

Ans. (a) The correct match is A-2, B-3, C-4, D-1.

14. Match the following.

List I (Types of Fracture)		List II (Meaning)
A.	Stress fracture	1. Bone breaks at a right angle.
B.	Transverse fracture	2. Splinter of bone into more than two fragments.
C.	Green Stick fracture	3. Bone bends and cracks.
D.	Comminuted fracture	4. Fatigued muscles transfers the overload of stress of the bone.

Codes

	A	B	C	D			A	B	C	D
(a)	4	1	3	2		(b)	2	3	1	4
(c)	1	3	4	2		(d)	3	4	2	1

Ans. (a) The correct match is A-4, B-1, C-3, D-2.

15. Match the following.

List I		List II
A.	Contusion	1. Treatment
B.	Green Stick	2. Skin damage
C.	Rice	3. Fracture
D.	Abrasion	4. Swelling

Codes

	A	B	C	D			A	B	C	D
(a)	4	3	1	2		(b)	3	4	2	1
(c)	2	3	1	4		(d)	1	2	3	4

Ans. (a) The correct match is A-4, B-3, C-1, D-2.

• Assertion and Reasoning

Directions (Q. Nos. 1-4) *Each of these questions contains two statements, Assertion (A) and Reason (R). Each of these questions also has four alternative choices, any one of which is the correct answer. You have to select one of the codes (a), (b), (c) and (d) given below.*

Codes
(a) Both A and R are true and R is the correct explanation of A
(b) Both A and R are true, but R is not the correct explanation of A
(c) A is true, but R is false
(d) A is false, but R is true

1. **Assertion (A)** Flexibility is the quality of the muscles, ligaments and tendons that enables the joints of the body to move easily through a complete range of movement.

Reason (R) More flexibility of the joints reduces movement of limbs.

Ans. (c) The assertion is true as flexibility provides elasticity that enables the joints to move easily through a range of movements.

Reason is false as greater flexibility ensures greater or increased movement of limbs. Thus, A is true, but R is false.

2. Assertion (A) Strength of movement produced by a muscle depends upon how close to the joint it is attached.

Reason (R) A muscle attached further away will produce a powerful movement than one attached to nearer the joint.

Ans. (d) The assertion is false as strength of a movement depends on the explosive power of the muscle used and physical fitness.

Reason is true as a powerful movement can be produced by a muscle the farther away it is to a joint due to increased locomotion. Thus, A is false, but R is true.

3. Assertion (A) Health and safety skills can be taught in the school through first-aid and safety education.

Reason (R) School age is the appropriate age to learn first-aid and safety education.

Ans. (a) The assertion is true as first-aid provides health and safety measures that can be taught to the students in school.

The reason is also true as school age is a tender age in which there can be maximum learning. Another reason is children can quickly learn first-aid as they usually fall or get hurt more often than adults. So, reason explains assertion completely. Thus, Both A and R are true and R is the correct of explanation of A.

4. Assertion (A) Basketball players face injuries due to overuse of joints.

Reason (R) Basketball players may get muscle, ligaments or tendon injuries as a result of repetitive stress.

Ans. (d) The assertion is false as there is no study that says that Basketball players face joint injuries due to its overuse.

The reason is true as muscle, ligament or tendon injuries may take place due to repetitive stress known as overuse injury in all the players including Basketball players. Thus, A is false, but R is true.

• Case Based MCQs

1. Early morning, we observe many older people following fitness regime. One day Ramu observed a 60-year-old man was holding his chest on the ground. When Ramu approached him he said that he felt chest pain regularly after jogging.

(i) What is the rate of normal heart beat of an adult?
(a) 72   (b) 80
(c) 65   (d) 90

Ans. (a) The rate of normal heart beat of an adult is 72.

(ii) Age and gender play a very important role in which of these components?
(a) Endurance   (b) Strength
(c) Explosive Strength   (d) Speed

Ans. (b) Age and gender play a very important role in strength.

(iii) Muscular strength starts receding during the age of
(a) 25-30 years   (b) 35-40 years
(c) 45-50 years   (d) 50-55 years

Ans. (b) Muscular strength starts receding during the age of 35-40 years.

2. Ramya and Deepthi were state level badminton players of our school. They used to practice hard even during off season. One day while practicing, due to lack of proper warm up, Ramya had injured her elbow and Deepthi had a sprain in her ankle joint. They were sent to hospital first-aid was administered. **(CBSE Question Bank 2021)**

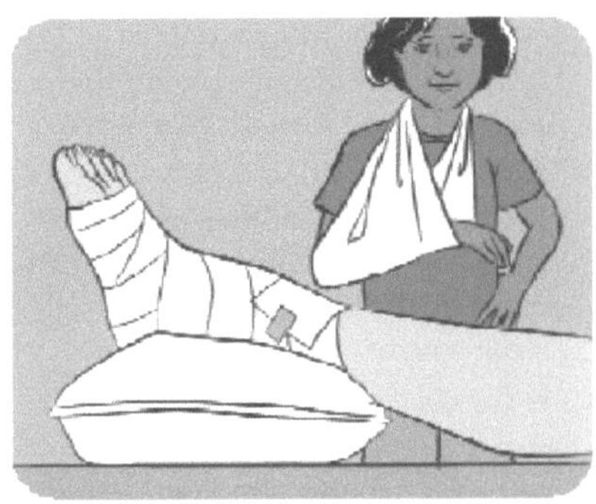

(i) Sprain is an injury caused to
(a) Bone   (b) Skin
(c) Ligament   (d) Muscle

Ans. (c) Sprain is an injury caused to a ligament.

(ii) The letter 'C' in PRICE stands
(a) Conduction   (b) Compression
(c) Concussion   (d) Contraction

Ans. (b) The letter 'C' in PRICE stands for compression which means to compress the affected area with a wrap or bandage.

(iii) The test to be conducted for bone injuries is
(a) X-ray   (b) Blood test
(c) ECG   (d) EEG

Ans. (a) The test that should be conducted for bone injuries is X-ray. The exact location and nature of damage is known through X-ray only.

Subjective Questions

• Short Answer (SA) Type Questions

1. Define physiology. Why physiology is important in sports?

Ans. Physiology is defined as the branch of science that deals with the functioning of the organs and their relationships with other organ systems to maintain functioning of human body.

Physiology is essential to understand how to attain physical fitness in order to enhance the performance in sports by improving the functions of the body.

It facilitates the profiling and monitoring of specific parameters relevant to optimise sports performance. Physiology is also important to understand sports activities alter the structure and functioning of our body.

2. Discuss the different factors that determine strength as a component of physical fitness

Ans. The factors determining strength as a component of physical fitness are as follows.

(i) **Size of the Muscle** The size of the muscle determines the strength possessed by an individual. Males have bigger and larger muscles due to which they have more strength than females.

(ii) **Muscle Composition** Muscles consist of two types of fibres i.e. fast twitch fibres (white fibres) and slow twitch fibres (red fibres). The fast twitch fibres are capable to contract faster and therefore they can produce more force.

On the contrary, the slow twitch fibres are not capable to contract faster but they are capable to control for a longer duration.

Muscles containing more percentage of fast twitch fibres produce more strength. The percentage of fast and slow twitch fibres is genetically determined and cannot be changed through training.

(iii) **Intensity of the Nerve Impulse** A muscle consists of many motor units. The number of contracting motor units determines the total force. If muscles contract with greater intensity then more strength will be produced.

3. Discuss the physiological factors determining flexibility.

Ans. The physiological factors determining flexibility are as follows

(i) **Joint Structure** The joint structure of a person determines the range of motions and hence level the flexibility of an individual.

For example, the ball and socket joint of the shoulder has the greatest range of motion in comparison to the knee joint.

(ii) **Age and Gender** The age of a person as well as the gender determines the level of flexibility. It can be enhanced with the help of training as strength and endurance are enhanced. Flexibility decreases with advancement of age and females are more flexible than males.

(iii) **Stretchability of Muscles** If the muscles are regularly stretched, then they remain flexible. The stretchability of muscles depends on the amount of exercises and physical activities.

4. Explain the difference between oxygen intake and oxygen uptake.

Ans. The difference between oxygen intake and oxygen uptake is given below

Oxygen Intake	Oxygen Uptake
It is the amount of oxygen which can be drawn into the lungs from the atmosphere.	It is the amount of oxygen which can be absorbed or consumed by the working muscles from the blood.
It depends upon size of the chest, strength of respiratory muscles, lung size, number of active alveoli, etc.	It depends on the rate of diffusion of oxygen into the blood, which is further determined by the speed of blood flow, blood temperature and the partial pressure of oxygen in blood.

5. Discuss three effects of exercise on the muscular system of our body.

Ans. The effects of exercise on the muscular system are as follows

(i) **Increase in Lactate Threshold** Exercise increases the ability of the muscles to tolerate lactic acid. This increases endurance as the working capacity of the muscles rises and muscles work for longer duration without fatigue.

(ii) **Increase in Muscle Mass** Regular exercise and physical activities increase the muscle mass of a person thus making him stronger, fitter and healthier.

(iii) **Muscle Coordination** Frequent exercise and special use of specific muscles for the same or similar skilled tasks, like dribbling a ball in a game of football leads to improved coordination. The coordination of nerves to the skeletal muscles also improves.

6. Explain the redistribution of blood flow in our body during exercise and rest.

Ans. During exercise the requirement of oxygen by the active muscles goes up by 10 to 12 times. From 1200 ml/minute at rest, it can go up to 12,500 ml/minute at maximal exercise. Similarly, the requirement of the skin goes up from 500 ml/minute to 1900 ml/minute during maximal exercise.

This increase can be accomplished through increased cardiac output and redistribution of blood from areas of the body like the kidneys, abdomen and other areas.

For instance, at rest the blood flow through the kidneys is 1100 ml/minute, which can be reduced to 600 ml/minute during exercise. Similarly, the blood flow at rest through the abdomen is 1400 ml/minute, which can be reduced to 600 ml/minute during exercise.

7. What are sports injuries? What are the two kinds of injuries?

Ans. A sports injury may be defined as "damage to the tissues of the body that occurs as a result of sport or exercise."

They are commonly caused by overuse, direct impact, or the application of force that is greater than the force that a body part can structurally withstand.

There are two kinds of sports injuries i.e. acute and chronic. Acute injury is a injury that occurs suddenly, such as sprained ankle caused by an awkward landing while, chronic injury is caused by repeated overuse of muscle groups or joints.

Poor technique and structural abnormalities can also contribute to the development of chronic injuries.

8. What is contusion? What are its causes and preventive measures?

Ans. A contusion is a bruise caused by a direct blow or repeated blows, crushing underlying muscle fibres and connective tissue without breaking the skin. It is common in boxing.

Contusion is caused due to repeated blows which causes accumulation of blood around the injury and it discolours the skin.

The preventive measures are that players should wear protective equipment. They should perform proper warm-ups. They should learn correct techniques, be cautious and alert.

9. What is the difference between laceration and incision? What first-aid should be used for treating them?

Ans. Laceration and incision are both a cut on the epidermis layer of skin due to a severe impact by a sharp object.

The difference is that, in laceration there is irregular break in the skin but in incision there is sharp, straight or diagonal cut on the skin.

The first-aid used for treating laceration/incision is

- Clean the surface of the cut with water.
- Apply antiseptic cream and bandage.
- If there is bleeding, then cover it with cotton or bandage and press to stop bleeding.

10. Explain briefly strain and sprain.

Ans. Strain and sprain are two common soft tissue injuries. Strain is caused due to twist, pull or tear of the muscles or tendons with symptoms of pain, swelling and loss of muscle strength.

On the other hand, sprain is a partial or complete tear of a ligament with symptoms of pain, swelling, bruising, loss of function. Both are caused due to weak muscular systems or insufficient warming up.

Strains often take place in the lower back region and back of the thigh area. Sprain usually takes place in the knee and ankle regions.

11. Mention briefly about the common sports injuries and their prevention. **(CBSE 2018)**

Ans. Some of the common sports injuries are abrasion, contusion, strain, sprain, fractures, dislocations, etc.

The two common injuries are as follows

(i) **Strain** It is defined as an injury to a tendon (tissues that connect your muscles and bones) or muscle. It often occurs in the lower back and in the muscle in the back of the thigh.

Prevention

Develop a balanced fitness program that incorporates cardiovascular exercises, strength, training and flexibility.

(ii) **Stress Fracture** It is an overuse injury. It occurs when muscles become fatigued and are unable to absorb added shock.

Prevention

Conditioning exercises during practice strengthens muscles.

12. What do you understand by fracture? Explain three first aid techniques for fractures.

Ans. Fracture is a bone injury that breaks the continuity of a bone or separates it into two or more parts.

The first aid techniques for fractures are as follows

- Immediately immobilise the injured area. Do not try to re-align the bone or push back in a bone that may be sticking out.
- Apply ice packs to limit swelling and help relieve pain until medical help arrives.
- Attempt to make the area as safe as possible by removing the patient from the danger and calling a specialist for help.

13. What do you understand by first-aid? Discuss briefly about the aims and objectives of first-aid. **(CBSE 2018)**

Ans. First-aid is the assistance given to any person suffering from a sudden illness or injury, with care provided to preserve life, prevent the condition from worsening and promote recovery.

Aims and objectives of first-aid are as follows

- Preserving life by carrying out emergency first aid procedures. It also includes first aider's life.
- Preventing the casualty's condition from deteriorating any further.
- Promoting recovery by arranging prompt emergency medical help.
- Provide relief to the wounded person from pain and suffering is another important objective of first aid.

14. Explain the first-aid procedure for minor wounds and cuts.

Ans. First-aid procedure for minor wounds and cuts are as follows

- Wash hands or wear sterile disposable gloves.
- Clean the surface of the cut or the wound with water.
- If there is a minor cut, then apply antiseptic cream or lotion to the affected part.
- If there is bleeding, then cover the wound with cotton or bandage and press to stop bleeding or raise the affected area above the heart level.
- If cut is deep then take to the doctor immediately for stitches.

• Long Answer (LA) Type Questions

1. What are the various factors affecting physiological fitness? Explain. **(All India 2015)**

Or Discuss the physiological factors determining components of physical fitness. **(Delhi 2015)**

Ans. Physiological factors determining components of physical fitness are as follows

(i) **Muscular Strength** This is the maximum force or tension a muscle or a muscle group can exert against a resistance. Physiologically, the muscle will increase in strength only if it has to increase its workload beyond what is ordinarily required of it.

(ii) **Speed** This is the rapidity with which one can repeat successive movements of the same pattern. Individuals with greater speed have superior reaction time.

(ii) **Endurance** This is the ability of a muscle or muscle group to perform repeated contractions against a resistance / load or to sustain contraction for an extended period of time with less discomfort and more rapid recovery.

(iv) **Flexibility** This is a quality of the muscles, ligaments and tendons that enables the joints of the body to move easily through a complete range of movement.

2. Discuss the factors determining speed.

Ans. The factors determining speed are discussed as follows

(i) **Bio-chemical Reserves and Metabolic Power** For maximum speed performance, the muscles require more amount of energy at a very high rate of consumption. For this work, the phosphagen Adenosine Triphosphate (ATP) and Creatine Phosphate (CP) stores in the muscles should be enough.

If ATP and CP store is less in contracting muscles, the muscle contractions due to insufficient energy supply become slow after a short time.

The metabolic power depends upon the energy supplied through certain enzymes. Proper working of the enzymes means high rate of metabolism which increases speed of doing work.

(ii) **Muscle Composition** Muscles consist of two types of fibres i.e. fast twitch fibres (white fibres) and slow twitch fibres (red fibres). A person containing more of fast twitch fibres will have greater speed.

(iii) **Mobility of the Nervous System** The rapid contraction and relaxation of the muscles takes place due to rapid excitation of the nervous system. The rapid movements give greater speed.

The nervous system can maintain this rapid excitation and inhibition only for a few seconds after which the excitation spreads to the neighbouring centres causing tension in the entire body. This results in decrease in speed.

3. What are the effects of exercising on the cardiorespiratory system? Explain. **(CBSE 2020)**

Or A trainer can improve the cardiorespiratory system with the help of exercise. Justify this statement.

Ans. The cardiorespiratory system consists of organs responsible for taking in oxygen for respiration and releasing carbon dioxide and water vapour, which are the waste products formed during respiration.

The passages in the nose, windpipe (trachea), bronchi, lungs and air sacs are the main organs of the respiratory system.

A trainer can improve the cardiorespiratory system with the help of exercise by

(i) **Decrease in Rate of Respiration** When a beginner starts exercise, then his rate of respiration increases. But when the same individual performs exercise daily, then his rate of respiration decreases in comparison to the beginning stage at rest.

(ii) **Lung Volume** For normal breathing at rest, lung expand and there is a change in air pressure. During exercise, due to rapid movement of diaphragm and intercostal muscles, total area of lung expands to accommodate more exchange of gases.

(iii) **Lung Diffusion Capacity** During exercise, the lung diffusion capacity increases in both trained and untrained persons. However, trained athletes may increase their diffusion capacity 30% more than that of an untrained person because athlete's lung surface area and red blood cell count is higher than that of non-athletes.

(iv) **Pulmonary Ventilation** The amount of air passing through lungs each minute is called Pulmonary Ventilation.

The Pulmonary Ventilation (PV) is a produced of Tidal Volume (TV) and Respiratory Rate (RR) and therefore at rest it is around 8 l/min.

During exercise time both TV and RR increase, due to which PV will also increase depending on the intensity of exercise. For an ordinary person, the value of PV may be 40-50 l/min and for well trained athlete, it may be around 100 l/min.

(v) **Residual Air Volume** It is the volume of air in the lungs which is left after exhalation. With exercises, the residual air capacity increases which enhances efficiency of lungs.

4. What do you understand by fracture? How can fractures be classified? Explain.

Ans. Fracture is defined as a loss of continuity in the substance of a bone. It is simply a break in the bone. It commonly happens because of accident, fall, or sport injuries. It is classified into different types, which are discussed as follows

(i) **Stress Fracture** A stress fracture is an overuse injury. It occurs when muscles become fatigued and are unable to absorb added shock. Eventually, the fatigued muscle transfers the overload of stress to the bone causing a tiny crack, called a stress fracture.

(ii) **Greenstick Fracture** A greenstick fracture occurs when a bone bends and cracks, instead of breaking completely into separate pieces. Most greenstick fractures occur in children younger than 10 years of age. This type of broken bone most commonly occur in children because their bones are softer and more flexible than are the bones of adults.

(iii) **Comminuted Fracture** It is a break or splinter of the bone into more than two fragments. Since considerable force and energy is required to fragment bone, fractures of this kind occurs after high-impact trauma such as vehicular accidents.

This type of fracture is usually challenging to treat because the break is so complex.

(iv) **Transverse Fracture** It is a fracture where the bone breaks at a right angle to the long axis of the bone. Transverse fractures most often occur as the result of strong force applied perpendicular to the long axis of a bone.

(v) **Oblique Fracture** An oblique fracture is characterised by a break that is curved or at an angle to the bone. A sharp blow that comes from an angle (i.e., above or below) may cause oblique fractures.

(vi) **Impacted Fracture** An impacted fracture is one whose ends are driven into each other. This commonly occurs with arm fractures in children and is sometimes known as a buckle fracture.

5. Write in detail about the dislocation and fractures among the bones and joint injuries.

Ans. The dislocation and fractures among the bones and joints happen when excessive force is applied directly or indirectly. These are musculoskeletal injuries and can be grouped under hard tissue injury.

A dislocation refers to displacement or separation of bones from the joint. It is caused by a sudden impact, a trauma or a fall.

A dislocated joint may be accompanied by numbness or tingling at the joint or beyond it. It is intensely painful, especially if you try to use joints or put weight on it. Some of the common joint injuries are shoulder dislocation, knee cap dislocation, finger dislocation etc. A fracture is a break in the continuity of a bone or a separation of a bone in two or more parts. It is caused when greater force is exerted against a bone than it can actually sustain. The different types of fractures are stress fracture, green stick, communated, transverse, oblique and impacted. The first aid is very essential in managing bone and joint injuries.

• Case Based Questions

1. On seeing a sharp cut on his friend's finger, Arun rushed with bandages and wipes. Imagining the scene in your mind, answer the following questions.

(i) Explain why you have chosen the answer in question (1)

Ans. Incision is the selected answer as it is a sharp cut on the skin that cuts into tissues, blood vessels, muscles or tendons. It can cause bleeding so Arun rushing with bandages and wipes show that it is an incision.

(ii) What kind of injury is Laceration?

Ans. Laceration is the tearing of the skin that results in an irregular wound. It is a soft tissue injury.

2. The Godavari School attended a CBSE Cluster Basketball Tournament. During the semi-final match Varun, one of the players fell down and was injured on the shoulder. He was immediately given first aid by the coach Mr. Rahul, who had the knowledge of first aid. Warm-up session is essential for players to avoid any serious injuries during the match.

(i) What do you mean by first-aid?

Ans. First-aid is the assistance given to any person suffering from a sudden illness or injury, with care provided to preserve life, prevent the condition from worsening and/or promote recovery.

(ii) Which type of sports injury is known as 'strain'? **(CBSE 2019)**

Ans. A strain is defined as an injury to a tendon or muscle. It often occurs in lower back and in thighs.

3. Mr. Raghav, aged 45 years was advised by his doctor to exercise regularly and take care of his dietary habbits. This advice was given keeping in view his advancing age and sedentary working profile. Considering his lifestyle answer the following questions

(i) What is stroke volume? **(All India 2016)**

Ans. The volume of blood pumped into the heart with every heartbeat is known as the stroke volume. In an untrained male, it is 50 to 70 ml/beat.

(ii) Explain the meaning of cardiac output. **(CBCE 2018)**

Ans. Cardiac output is the term that describes the amount of blood your heart pumps each minute.

Chapter Test

Multiple Choice Questions

1. _____ is a shallow wound, typically wearing away of the top layer of skin (the epidermis) due to an applied friction force against the body.

   (a) Contusion   (b) Abrasion

   (c) Laceration   (d) Incision

2. _____ is defined as an injury to a tendon or muscle.

   (a) Contusion   (b) Incision

   (c) Sprain   (d) Strain

3. Which of the following is not an objective of first-aid?

   (a) To preserve life

   (b) To prevent deterioration

   (c) To promote recovery

   (d) None of the above

4. Which of the following statements is not correct?

   (a) Functioning of cardiorespiratory system increases with exercise.

   (b) Weak muscles limit the range of movements.

   (c) Long term training programme increases the resting heart rate.

   (d) Muscle size gets affected by the intensity of exercises.

5. Shradha was a state level Badminton player. One day while practicing, she badly injured her knee and had a sprain in the ankle too. Here coach immediately sent her to the hospital for a knee check up as he suspected a fracture or a dislocation

   The type of injury in the knee is _____

   (a) Dislocation   (b) Abrasion

   (c) Laceration   (d) Incision

Short Answer (SA) Type Questions

6. Anatomical factors, age and equipment may cause sports injuries. Explain.

7. List 3 steps for the prevention of sports injuries related to Abrasion

8. Explain three factors that affect the flexibility of the people.

9. Compare the basis on which different type of sports injuries are classified.

10. What is dislocation? Briefly describe the different types of dislocation.

Long Answer (LA) Type Questions

11. Discuss the short term effects of exercises on muscles.

12. Enumerate the effects of exercises on cardio respiratory system.

Answers

1. (b)   *2.* (d)   *3.* (d)   *4.* (c)   *5.* (c)

CHAPTER 04

Psychology and Sports

In this Chapter...

- Personality and its types
- Big Five Theory
- Motivation
- Aggression in Sports

The word 'psychology' refers to 'a study of human behaviour' and sports psychology is a sub-category of psychology that deals with the behaviour of the athletes and teams engaged in competitive sports.

Sports psychology plays a vital role in enhancing the performance of players to a great extent. Psychological factors like learning, interest, attitude, motivation, emotion, stress, etc., largely affects the performance of players.

Therefore, the knowledge of psychology helps the physical educators and the coaches to understand the behaviour of players and how desirable changes and modifications can be brought in their behavioural pattern to improve the level of their performance.

Personality

The word 'personality' is derived from Latin word *'persona'* which means a *'mask'*. Actors in ancient Greece used to wear these masks when they acted in plays. Thus, removing the masks means showing your true self or your identity.

Personality is basically a set of characteristics like attitude, habits, traits, etc., possessed by a person which greatly influence his motivation, emotion and behaviour in different situations. It reveals the psychological make up of an individual through his behaviour.

Some definitions of personality are as follows

According to **NL Munn**, "Personality is the most characteristic integration of an individual's structure, mode of interest, attitude, behaviour, capacities, abilities and aptitudes."

According to **Ogburn and Nimkoff**, "The totality of sentiments, attitudes, ideas, habits, skills and behaviours of an individual is personality."

According to **JP Guildford**, "Personality is an individual's unique pattern of traits which distinguishes one individual from the other."

Types of Personality

The types of personality on the basis of physical attributes were given by **Herbert Sheldon** and on the basis of mental attribute was given by **Carl Jung**. These are discussed as follows

Personality Types According to Herbert Sheldon

Sheldon distinguished the personality on the basis of physical attributes like bodyshape, temperament, etc.

1. Endomorph

Endomorphs have a pear-shaped and rounded physique. They have short arms and legs. The upper parts of the arms and legs seems to be thicker than the lower parts. They have underdeveloped muscles.

Generally, they are more prone to become obese. Their excessive mass hinders their ability to compete in sports.

These are most suitable for activities in which great strength is required. Sports like weight- lifting and power-lifting are most suitable for endomorphs.

2. Ectomorph

Ectomorphs are usually referred to as slim persons because their muscles and limbs are elongated. Usually, they have lot of difficulties in gaining weight. They have flat chest and have less muscles mass.

They do not have a lot of strength but they dominate the endurance sports as their body type is naturally suited to perform wonderfully in endurance sports. They are best suited for games and sports like gymnastics.

3. Mesomorph

They are somewhere between endomorph and ectomorph. They have broad shoulders, narrow waist (wedge shaped), muscular body, strong limbs and average body fat.

They are well proportioned. They are physically capable of doing a lot of activities and tend to be athletically aggressive. They are adventurous, energetic and competitive.

They have enough strength, speed and agility due to which they can excel in sports which require great strength, short bursts of energy and lots of power. Mesomorph people take off or put on weights easily.

Personality Types According to Carl Jung

Carl C Jung distinguished people according to the nature and attitude of the person. The types are described as follows

Extroverts-Introverts

This represents a person's direction of energy expression. An extrovert is more open as the direction of energy is derived and expressed in the external world, environment and surroundings. Therefore, they are talkative, sociable, action-oriented, friendly and out-going.

On the other hand, an introvert is mainly confined to internal world i.e. his ownself and therefore is not so open, less talkative, etc.

Apart from these two, there is another type i.e. Ambiverts. An ambivert person has a balance of extrovert and introvert features in their personality.

Sensing-Intuition

This represents the way by which a person perceives information. Sensing means that the person perceives information that he receives through the senses or external world.

On the other hand, intuition (natural instinct) means that the person believes mainly information that he receives through the inner-self or imaginary world.

Thinking-Feeling

This represents the way a person processes information. Thinking means a person processes or makes a decision by logical reasoning.

On the other hand, feeling means that a person processes information based on emotions.

Judging-Perceiving

This represents the way how a person implements the information that has been processed. Judging means moving in a systematic manner by organising the life's events according to the plans made.

On the other hand, perceiving means exploring alternative options or moving spontaneously at times without much planning.

Personality Traits (Big Five Theory)

Personality trait refers to the quality or characteristics that describe a personality. There are five personality traits that are described in 'Big Five Theory'.

These are openness, conscientiousness, extraversion, agreeableness and neuroticism which are also referred as OCEAN.

These traits are discussed as follows

1. **Openness** Its characteristics are imagination and insight. People high on this trait are creative, adventurous and have a broad range of interests. They are open to change.

2. **Conscientiousness** Its characteristics include high level of thoughtfulness, good impulse control and goal-directed behaviours.

   People high on this trait are reliable, organised and mindful of details. The trait determines discipline, management as well as risk taking ability.

3. **Extroversion** It is characterised by sociability, assertiveness and high amount of emotional expressiveness. Extroversion shows how social a person is, or how loving, caring and warm.

These people love to go out and party. The extroversion includes traits like being energetic, talkative and assertive.

4. **Agreeableness** This includes attributes like trust, kindness, affection and other social behaviours. People high in this trait are cooperative, dependable, trustworthy and caring.

5. **Neuroticism** Its characteristics are sadness, moodiness and emotional instability. People high in this trait experience mood swings, anxiety, irritability, negative emotions and sadness. They tend to be worrisome, preoccupied and anxious.

Modern Day Types of Personality

Nowadays, the personality has four basic types. These are given as follows

Personality Type A These personalities are described as competitive and high achievers. They have high sense of time and always try to finish their job in time. They are always found busy. They can be easily aroused to anger, hostility and aggression.

Personality Type B These personalities are extrovert in nature. They are very entertaining and not easily stressed. They express their emotions appropriately and cope with stress effectively.

They can be achievers but still they do not want to be competitive. They can delay the work and try to do at the last moment.

Personality Type C These personalities try to spend a lot of time on finding about how the things work. They are very cautious and reserved in nature. They are interested in accuracy, rationality and logic.

They are not assertive and always suppress their own desires and emotions. They are more susceptible to depression as compared to type A and type B.

Personality Type D They have a negative outlook towards life and are pessimistic. They are characterised as those people who resist any form of change and prefer the monotony of routine.

They are not adventurous and always resist responsibility. The repetition allows them to become very skilled.

They withdraw as a result of fear of rejection. The main cause of depression is suppressing the emotions for long periods of time.

Role of Sports in Personality Development

Sports help in the overall development of a person. It develops a person mentally as well as physically. Participation in sports and physical activities enhances the personality of a person.

When a person is physically fit and mentally strong, then automatically it reflects in vibrant personality.

Role of sports can be explained as follows

1. **Development of Physique** A good physique can be developed by regular training and participating in sports. A well-built physique exhibits good personality that is attractive and impressive.

2. **Social Skills** Sports help in developing social skills as players play together, bond with each other, share their problems and worries as well as cooperate with each other.

3. **Relieve Stress** Stress can be relieved by playing any type of sport. Sports help persons to combat anxiety, depression and stress. When the stress is relieved, it improves the personality of the persons.

4. **Discipline** Sports help in making a person disciplined as it is essential to practise and then complete all the tasks on time without fear of failure. This helps in making of a good personality.

5. **Leadership Quality** Sports help in developing leadership quality as it provides opportunities to the players to lead. The personality of an individual is enhanced by improved leadership qualities.

6. **Builds Confidence** Sports help in developing confidence as players need to interact with each other, make their move, take quick decisions, etc. This helps in developing mental ability and builds confidence.

7. **Builds Self-esteem** A person in sports acquires various skills and qualities like confidence, leadership, good decision- making, agility, etc. This develops high self-esteem which is an important personality trait.

8. **Planning** In sports, players plan their actions and moves. This inculcates good organisation and planning skills which help in the overall personality development.

Motivation

The word motivation is derived from a Latin word *'movere'* which means *'to move '*. Motivation means that one is driven or moved by an inner urge or force to achieve the goal.

It means an inspiration to do or achieve something. It is a psychological tool that arouses feeling in a person to achieve his/her goal.

A player working hard to win a gold medal is said to be motivated. Sometimes people motivate others by different ways such as elders giving rewards to their children to do well in exams, etc.

Motivation is implicit in every function of life. For example, simple acts like eating and drinking are motivated by hunger and thirst respectively.

Some definitions of motivation are as follows

According to **Atkinson**, "The term 'motivation' refers to the arousal of tendency to act, to produce one or more effects."

According to **Johnson**, "Motivation is the influence of general pattern of activities indicating and directing the behaviour of the organism."

Hence, from the above definitions we can say that, motivation is an inner feeling which prompt a person to work more in a right direction towards attainment of goals.

Types of Motivation

A person who has a high level of motivation is likely to perform better and show excellence as compared to the one who is not motivated or less motivated.

There are two types of motivation *i.e.* intrinsic and extrinsic which are discussed as follows

1. **Internal Motivation or Intrinsic Motivation** This motivation is within an individual and guides one to perform better to satisfy one's own personal feelings.

   In other words, it means the individual's motivational stimuli are coming from within. The individual has the desire to perform a specific task, because its results are in accordance with his belief system or fulfills a desire.

2. **External Motivation or Extrinsic Motivation** This motivation depends upon external factors such as a reward given by a parent, school awards, punishments, etc.

   Here, an individual is motivated not from within but somebody inspires that person. Extrinsic motivation can be positive or negative and produces lot of behavioural changes.

Techniques of Motivation

Following are the techniques of motivation

1. **Knowledge of the Goal** It is one of the most important techniques of motivation. A person should be made aware about the attainment of the goal.

   The player should be acquainted well with the aim and objectives of the goal.

   For example, telling the player that the goal is to cover 100 m distance in shortest time. In this, knowledge of goal helps the player to reach towards it.

2. **Rewards** Announcing rewards that will be given, once the tasks are accomplished successfully, has a great effect on a person's performance.

   For example, parents giving chocolates to their children for good performance.

Rewards are of various types and help in achieving the goal, like cash, prize, job, professional security, honour, social status, etc. The rewards should be presented in front of all recipients.

3. **Punishment** Punishment is of various types like physical punishment, blame, economical punishment, social withdrawal, etc.

   It is a type of negative motivation in which a person is shown fear, so that he works for better results. However, it should be avoided as much as possible.

4. **Active Participation** Active involvement of the coach/teacher develops healthy competition and interaction between the students. Teachers are able to identify the problems and explain how to solve those problems.

5. **Test-evaluations and Competitions** These methods help us to know our abilities, deficiencies and comparison of performance (in relation to others). These act as feedback to overcome our deficiencies and improve further.

6. **Equipment and Surroundings** Modern equipment and healthy surroundings like well maintained playgrounds, latest sports equipments, etc., act as motivating factors for high performance.

7. **Teaching Methods** An effective teaching method directly influences the performance of a person. The teacher acts as a motivator, to improve the performance of the students.

   For this, the teachers should be aware of the latest technology.

8. **Discussion** Healthy and constructive discussion is very essential for motivation. It ensures proper motivation to a player for attainment of specified goal or objective. It also reveals what type of motivation should be given to team or players to attain desired performance.

9. **Competition** In games and sports, competition works as the best motivator. Every sportsperson tries to give his best with optimum efforts to raise his performance level. Such type of competition is called individual competition. Team competition also works as a good motivating factor.

10. **Healthy Sports Environment** Providing a healthy sports environment will be a vital factor to enhance sports performance. It consists of good quality of sports equipment, coach, smooth and clean sports fields and other facilities.

11. **Positive Attitude** It enhances the level of intrinsic motivation and helps in accepting external motivation. Sportsperson with positive attitude gives his/her best to win the game.

Such people always show confidence in themselves despite having difficult situations. Coaches and trainers also play an important role in imparting positive attitude.

On the other side, sportspersons with negative attitude are not able to perform well. They show less confidence and have mindset that they are inferior from their competitors.

12. **Spectators** These are good source of external motivation. When there are large number of spectators, then players get extra energy to perform well. Contrary to it, if there are very less spectators in the stadium, then players feel demotivated.

Effectiveness of presence of huge spectators depends upon the experience and maturity of athletes. An inexperienced athlete may not be able to perform better infront of huge spectators, in comparison to an experienced athlete.

Aggression

Aggression or aggressiveness means the intention to cause mental or physical harm to oneself, others or objects in the environment. This is done by doing physical harm, showing unkind or nasty behaviour, abusing or using words.

A person shows aggression due to stress, anger or even due to insecurity. Aggression may come instantly or may build up over time. It can be positive as well as negative.

Infact, some psychologists agreed upon the fact that aggression can enhance sports performance while some views it as a negative psychological characteristic.

According to **Baron and Richardsons**, "Any form of behaviour towards the goal of harming or injuring another living being who is motivated to avoid such treatment is aggression."

Concept of Aggression in Sports

In sports, aggression is often seen in the field, where players play aggressively. There is a desire to excel which leads to development of aggressiveness in player. So, aggression is positive when players play within the rules of the game with high intensity and without harming other players.

For example, in cricket, if a batsman is not able to hit the ball, then, he can scold oneself. This aggression will act as a intrinsic motivation.

However, aggression becomes negative when players have an intention to harm other players, use abusive language or do such things which are not within the laws of the game.

For example, pushing another player in a game of football or using abusive language for other players or teams.

Types of Aggression in Sports

In sports, aggression has been categorised into three kinds or types. These are instrumental aggression, hostile aggression and assertive behaviour, which are as follows

Instrumental Aggression

In instrumental aggression, the main aim is to achieve a goal by using aggression. It is a positive form of aggression. Here, the aim of the player is to excel in the sport that he is playing through high intensity output and competitive spirit.

For example, a football player using aggression to tackle his opponent and win the ball. He is not harming any player but only using his aggressiveness to gain the ball.

Experienced players show instrumental aggression on the field as they have greater self-control to manage their aggression.

Hostile Aggression

In hostile aggression, the main aim is to cause harm or injury to your opponent. It is usually an unplanned, impulsive reaction towards a player who may or have become a threat in achieving the goal. However, it may also be planned to cause injury to intended player on the field. This kind of aggression often arises from insult, hurt, bad feelings, jealousy and threat.

For example, a bowler throwing a bouncer to deliberately injure the batsman or to shake up his concentration.

In some extreme cases, hitting an opponent or deliberately obstructing his path leads to his fall on the ground.

This kind of aggression is usually seen in new players who want to achieve success quickly. The difference between the two is that instrumental aggression is positive where the aim is to excel by own efforts while hostile aggression is negative. Here, the aim is to excel by causing harm to others.

Assertive Behaviour

It is also referred as **assertive aggression**. It is generally seen as a positive form of aggression. In ground, it simply mean to stand up for your values in an unthreatening manner and involves the use of legitimate physical or verbal force to achieve one's goals.

For an act to be assertive, it must be goal directed with no specific intention to harm alongwith the use of legitimate force with no rules broken.

Thus, assertive behaviour should include four components *viz.* it should be goal oriented, should not be intended to harm, should use only legitimate force and should not break any rule of the sport.

Chapter Practice

Objective Questions

• Multiple Choice Questions

1. Endomorphic, Mesomorphic and Ectomorphic are types of _______.
(a) Bones
(b) Joints
(c) Personalities
(d) Muscles

Ans. (c) Endomorphic, Mesomorphic and Ectomorphic are types of personality on the basis of physical attributes like body shape, temperament, etc., given by Sheldon.

2. Traits like insight, imagination, receptivity towards new ideas are involved with _______.
(a) Openness
(b) Conscientiousness
(c) Agreeableness
(d) Extroversion

Ans. (a) Traits like insight, imagination, receptivity towards new ideas are involved with openness. People high on this trait are adventurous and have broad range of interest.

3. If an individual is moved by internal or external forces towards the goal, it is known as _______.
(a) Goal setting
(b) Outer forces
(c) Motivation
(d) Personality development

Ans. (c) An individual moved by internal or external forces towards the goal is said to be motivated. Motivation is the urge or force to achieve a goal.

4. The source of intrinsic motivation is _______.
(a) Teachers
(b) Family
(c) Self
(d) Siblings

Ans. (c) The source of intrinsic motivation is the self that refers to oneself, one's own interest, feelings, goals and targets.

5. Any physical behaviour intentionally aimed to harm others is known as _______ .
(a) Hostile aggression
(b) Instrumental aggression
(c) Negative aggression
(d) Assertive aggression

Ans. (a) Any physical behaviour intentionally aimed to harm others is known as Hostile aggression, eg. pushing insulting and hitting etc.

6. Which of the following is a trait of the personality shown below?

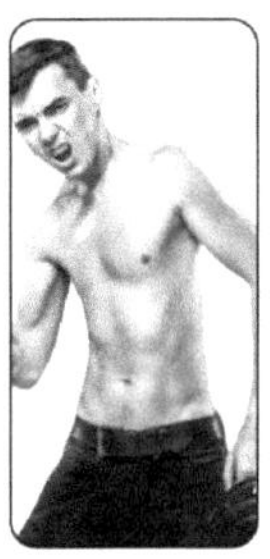

(a) Underdeveloped muscles
(b) Elongated limbs
(c) Muscular body
(d) None of the above

Ans. (b) The personality shown in the image in Ectomorph. Their personality trait is elongated limbs, difficulty in gaining weight, less muscle mass, etc.

7. Endomorphic people are ____. (CBSE 2020)
(a) Obese
(b) Energetic
(c) Solid Body
(d) Adventures

Ans. (a) Endomorphic people are obese.

8. Match the following.

	List I		List II
A.	Personality Type A	1.	Cautious and Reserved
B.	Personality Type B	2.	Competitive and High Achievers
C.	Personality Type C	3.	Extrovert and Achievers
D.	Personality Type D	4.	Pessimistic

Codes

	A	B	C	D			A	B	C	D
(a)	4	3	2	1		(b)	2	3	1	4
(c)	1	2	3	4		(d)	3	4	2	1

Ans. (b) The correct match is A-2, B-3, C-1, D-4.

9. Match the following.

List I	List II
(Personality Traits)	(Characteristics)
A. Openness	1. Assertive
B. Extroversion	2. Emotional
C. Neuroticism	3. Reliable
D. Conscientiousness	4. Creative

Codes

	A	B	C	D			A	B	C	D
(a)	3	2	1	4		(b)	1	3	4	2
(c)	2	4	3	1		(d)	4	1	2	3

Ans. (d) The correct match is A-4, B-1, C-2, D-4

10. Match the following.

List I	List II
A. Sensing	1. Perceiving
B. Extroverts	2. Intuition
C. Judging	3. Feeling
D. Thinking	4. Introverts

Codes

	A	B	C	D			A	B	C	D
(a)	3	4	2	1		(b)	2	4	1	3
(c)	1	3	4	2		(d)	2	4	3	1

Ans. (b) The correct match is A-2, B-4, C-1, D-3

11. Amit is a student of class X. He has a pear shaped body and rounded physique. He has short and thick arms and legs. He does not like to take part in any physical activity or sports.

Based on the case, answer the following question. Amit is having a personality of

(a) Endomorph

(b) Mesomorph

(c) Ectomorph

(d) None of the above

Ans. (a) Amit has short and thick arms, rounded physique which means that he has endomorph personality. These type of people do not take much interest in sports.

12. Different psychologists have given different types of personality on the basis of physical, mental attitude and personality traits. Traits refer to the quality or characteristics that describe personality.

Which of the following is the example of Trait Theory of personality?

(a) Sheldon's classification (b) Jung Classification

(c) Personality (d) Intrinsic

Ans. (b) Jung classification is the example of Trait Theory of personality which is given by Carl C Jung.

13. Rohit lost in the finals of Badminton championships held in his school. He got disappointed and stopped talking to anyone. He didn't meet even his friends. His coach advised his parents to take him to a psychologist so that he can understand Rohit's problem and provide solutions to cope up.

Taking help of psychologist becomes _______ kind of motivation.

(a) Intrinsic (b) Extrinsic

(c) Ambivert (d) Both (a) and (b)

Ans. (b) Taking help of psychologist becomes extrinsic kind of motivation e.g. Meeting a psychologist to solve emotional problem and negative feelings of frustration, disappointment, etc.

14. In the 'Big Five Theory', five personality traits are described. These traits are the attributes that describe a person. The traits given in Big Five Theory are collectively called as OCEAN.

What does A stands in OCEAN?

(a) Amiable (b) Adorable

(c) Agreeableness (d) Aggression

Ans. (c) A stands for agreeableness in OCEAN. The Big Five Theory classifies personalities on the basis of quality. O is for openness, C is for conscientiousness, E is for extroversion, A is for agreeableness and N is for neuroticism.

• Assertion and Reasoning MCQs

Directions (Q. Nos. 1-4) *Each of these questions contains two statements, Assertion (A) and Reason (R). Each of these questions also has four alternative choices, any one of which is the correct answer. You have to select one of the codes (a), (b), (c) and (d) given below.*

Codes

(a) Both A and R are true and R is the correct explanation of A

(b) Both A and R are true, but R is not the correct explanation of A

(c) A is true, but R is false

(d) A is false, but R is true

1. Assertion (A) Personality trait refers to the quality or characteristics that describe a personality.

Reason (R) In Big Five Theory, five personality traits are described.

Ans. (b) The assertion is true as the characteristics or qualities of a person define and describe a person. They are also called traits.

The reason is also true as Big Five Theory describes the five personality traits. But reason does not explain assertion clearly. Thus, Both A and R true, but R is not the correct explanation of A.

2. Assertion (A) Ectomorphs are individuals who have short leg and arms.

Reason (R) Emotional stability is an essential part of an individual's personality.

Ans. (d) Assertion is false as ectomorphs have elongated limbs and endomorphs have short legs and arms.

Reason is true as a person is stable only when he/she is emotionally stable and an emotionally stable person forms a balanced personality. Thus, A is false, but R is true.

3. Assertion (A) Carl C. Jung distinguished people according to nature and attitude of the person.

Reason (R) People high in neuroticism have high level of thoughtfulness and can be distinguished according to nature and attitude.

Ans. (c) Assertion is true as Carl C. Jung, has given the personality types based on the nature and attitudes of the people.

Reason is false as neuroticism relates to sadness, moodiness and emotional instability. Thus, A is true, but R is false.

4. Assertion (A) A person with high level of motivation is likely to perform better in sports.

Reason (R) Internal motivation guides one to perform better to satisfy one's own personal feelings.

Ans. (b) Assertion is true as a motivated person will give his/her best performance.

Reason is also true as internal or intrinsic motivation gives an individual a desire to perform a specific task with greater efficiency to satisfy one's own personal feelings. Thus, both A and R are true, but R is not the correct explanation of A.

• Case Based MCQs

1. Rohit studies in class X. He has elongated limbs and is very slim. He cannot pick up weight due to less muscle mass. Based on the case answer the following questions.

(i) Rohit is having a personality type of
(a) Endomorph
(b) Ectomorph
(c) Mesomorph
(d) None of the above

Ans. (b) Rohit is having a personality type of ectomorphs. Ectomorphs have elongated limbs, have less muscle mass and have slim bodies.

(ii) Due to his body type, he is naturally suited for which type of sports?
(a) Endurance type of sports
(b) Strength type of sports
(c) Speed type of sports
(d) Both (a) and (c)

Ans. (a) Due to ectomorph body type, Rohit is naturally suited for endurance type of sports. As he has less body fat, he has smaller body surface which suits him for endurance activity.

(iii) Which among the following sports/games is best suited for Rohit?
(a) Cricket　　　　　　　(b) Weight-lifting
(c) Chess　　　　　　　(d) Gymnastics

Ans. (d) The game best suited for Rohit is gymnastics due to his light body constitution. It makes him suitable for aerobic activity.

2. Rohan was a good athlete of our school. He used to undergo training regularly for the best results. In spite of his constant effort he could not succeed. He got frustrated with his poor performance and stopped expressing his feelings and meeting friends. His parents took him to a psychologist for help. After a few consultations, he was able to focus well and succeeded.　　　(CBSE Question Bank 2021)

(i) Rohan can be motivated using
(a) blame
(b) praise
(c) recognition
(d) Both (b) and (c)

Ans. (b) Rohan can be motivated using praise. Praise is a form of extrinsic motivation technique. It can boost good feelings and inspire children.

(ii) Taking help of a psychologist becomes kind of motivation.
(a) intrinsic　　　　　　(b) extrinsic
(c) ambivert　　　　　　(d) Both (a) and (b)

Ans. (b) Taking help of a psychologist is a kind of extrinsic motivation as this kind of motivation is driven by external rewards, external encouragement and guidance.

(iii) Pick the odd one out.
(a) Openness　　　　　　(b) Extroversion
(c) Neuroticism　　　　　(d) Ambivert

Ans. (d) Ambivert is the odd one out as it is not one of the personality traits of Big Five Theory. The personality traits of Big Five Theory are openness, conscientiousness, extroversion, agreeableness and neuroticism.

Subjective Questions

• Short Answer (SA) Type Questions

1. What is the role of psychology in sports?

Ans. Psychology plays a vital role in enhancing the performance of players to a great extent. Psychological factors like learning, interest, attitude, motivation, emotion, stress, etc., largely affects the performance of players. With the help of psychology, players as well as instructors can understand the weak areas and devise ways to bring improvement.

Therefore, the knowledge of psychology helps the physical educators and the coaches to understand the behaviour of players and how desirable changes and modifications can be brought in their behavioural pattern to improve the level of their performance.

2. Explain the meaning of personality with the help of definitions.

Ans. Personality is basically a set of characteristics like attitude, habits, traits, etc., possessed by a person which greatly influence his motivation, emotion and behaviour in different situations. It reveals the psychological make up of an individual through his behaviour.

Personality is a dynamic and continuous process of learning in which an individual acquires different psychological characteristics. The word 'personality' is also used to represent all the factors inherited or acquired, which make up an individual.

Some definitions of personality are as follows

According to Warren, "Personality is the entire organisation of a human being at any stage of development."

According to Guildford, "Personality is an individual's unique pattern of traits which distinguishes one individual from the other."

3. What are the types of personality as given by Sheldon?

Or Discuss the Sheldon types of personality in detail.

(CBSE 2020)

Ans. The personality type on the basis of physical attributes is given by William Herbert Sheldon. These are as follows

(i) **Endomorphs** They have a pear-shaped and rounded physique. They have short arms and legs. They are more inclined to become obese.

They are most suitable for activities in which great strength is required. Sports like weight-lifting and power-lifting are most suitable for endomorphs.

(ii) **Ectomorphs** They are usually referred to as slim persons because their muscles and limbs are elongated. They have great difficulty in gaining weight.

They have flat chest and have less muscle mass. They are best suited for games and sports like gymnastics.

(iii) **Mesomorphs** They are somewhere between endomorph and ectomorph.

They have broad shoulders, narrow waist (wedge shaped), muscular body, strong limbs and average body fat.

They are well proportioned. They are physically capable of doing a lot of activities and tend to be athletically aggressive. They are adventurous, energetic and competitive.

4. Write any three personality types that are formulated by Carl Jung.

Ans. The types that are formulated by Carl Jung are described as follows

(i) **Extroverts-Introverts** An extrovert is more open as the direction of energy is derived and expressed in the external world, environment and surroundings.

On the other hand, an introvert is mainly confined to internal world.

(ii) **Sensing-Intuition** Sensing means that the person perceives information that he receives through the senses or external world.

On the other hand, intuition means that the person believes mainly the information that he receives through the inner self or imaginery world.

(iii) **Thinking-Feeling** Thinking means a person processes or makes a decision by logical reasoning.

On the other hand, feeling means that a person processes information based on emotions.

5. Differentiate between Extroverts and Introverts.

Ans. The differences between extroverts and introverts are as follows

	Extroverts	Introverts
(i)	They are very social outgoing, confident, lively and make friends easily.	They are reserved, too self-conscious and more interested in their own thoughts and ideas.
(ii)	Actors politician group leaders are extroverts.	Poets, artists, writers, philosophers are introverts usually.
(iii)	Extroverts are more open as the direction of energy is derived and expressed in external world.	Introverts are mainly confined to their internal world i.e. their ownself.

6. Extrinsic motivation may sometimes kill intrinsic motivation Justify?

Ans. Intrinsic motivation is within an individual and guides him to perform better. It is based upon needs, interest, nature, emotions, social needs etc.

Sometimes extrinsic motivation may kill intrinsic motivation because the physical appearance of something i.e. reward or punishments has more influence on the mind of an athlete than his own desire to succeed. Therefore, it is important to encourage students to achieve excellence rather than rely on rewards and punishments only.

7. What is meant by motivation? Explain any two techniques of motivation for higher achievement in sports. **(All India 2017)**

Ans. Motivation means a process through which an individual is inspired or stimulated to act in a particular fashion or manner towards a particular direction. Techniques of motivation for higher achievement in sports are as follows

(i) **Active Participation** Active involvement of the coach/teacher develops healthy competition and interaction between the students. Teachers are able to identify the problems and explain how to solve those problems.

(ii) **Rewards** Announcing rewards that will be given, once the tasks are completed successfully, has a great effect on a person's performance.

For example, parents giving chocolates to their children for good performance. Rewards are of various types and help in achieving the goal, like cash, prize, job, professional security, honour, social status, etc.

8. Discuss in detail any three techniques of motivation. **(CBSE 2020)**

Ans. The three techniques of intrinsic motivation are as follows

(i) **Knowledge of the Goal** It is one of the most important techniques of motivation. A person should be made aware about the attainment of the goal. The player should be acquainted well with the aim and objectives of the goal.

For example, telling the player that the goal is to cover 100 m distance in shortest time. In this, knowledge of the goal helps the player to reach towards it.

(ii) **Equipment and Surroundings** Modern equipment and healthy surroundings like well maintained playgrounds, latest sports equipments, etc., act as motivating factors for high performance.

(iii) **Positive Attitude** Positive attitude enhances the level of intrinsic motivation and helps in accepting external motivation. Sportsperson with positive attitude gives his/her best to win its game.

Such people always show confidence in themselves despite having difficult situations. Coaches and trainers also play an important role in imparting positive attitude.

9. What are the types of aggression? **(CBSE 2020)**

Ans. There are three types of aggression in sports. They are as follows

(i) **Instrumental Aggression** The main aim is to achieve a goal by using aggression. For example, a footballer using aggression to tackle his opponent by high intensity play without harming anyone.

(ii) **Hostile Aggression** The main aim is to cause harm or injury to the opponent. It is usually unplanned, impulsive reaction. For example, a bowler throwing a bouncer to deliberately injure the batsman.

(iii) **Assertive Behaviour** It is also referred as assertive aggression. It is generally seen as a positive form of aggression. In ground, it simply means to stand up for your values in an unthreatening manner, and involves the use of legitimate physical or verbal force to achieve once's goals.

10. Explain Assertive behaviour in detail.

Ans. Assertive behaviour is also referred as assertive aggression. It is generally seen as a positive form of aggression. In ground, it simply means to stand up for your values in an unthreatening manner, and involves the use of legitimate physical or verbal force to achieve one's goals.

For an act to be assertive, it must be goal directed with no specific intention to harm along with the use of legitimate force with no rules broken.

Thus, assertive behaviour should include four components *viz.* it should be goal-oriented, should not be intended to harm, should use only legitimate force and should not break any rule of the sport.

11. Why players show hostile aggression on the field?

Ans. Players who want to achieve success quickly or are not able to manage their emotions, show hostile aggression towards another player.

Sometimes players loose their self-control or are not able to manage humiliation and feel hurt and insulted, then they show hostile aggression as a form of revenge. Usually, new players show greater hostility than experienced players. Such aggression is against the spirit of the game. Hostile aggression may also arise as a result of bad feelings, jealousy, insecurity and threat. Here, the aim is to harm the player who becomes the reason for bad feelings. However, hostile aggression may be planned or unplanned to cause injury to the intended player on the field.

12. Distinguish between instrumental and hostile aggression.

Ans. The difference between instrumental and hostile aggression are as follows

	Instrumental Aggression	Hostile Aggression
(i)	It is a positive kind of aggression as aim is to achieve a goal/target.	It is a negative kind of aggression as aim is to cause harm or injury to others.
(ii)	It arises from the need to excel and to do better.	It arises from insult, hurt bad feelings, jealousy and threat.
(iii)	Here, the aim is to excel by improving their own performance.	Here, the aim is to excel but by devising ways to reduce the performance of others.
(iv)	For example, a footballer using aggression to tackle his opponent by high intensity play without harming anyone.	For example, a boller throwing a bouncer to deliberately injure the batsman.

• Long Answer (LA) Type Questions

1. Explain the structure of personality. Describe the role of sports in developing the personality.

(Delhi 2016)

Ans. The word 'personality' is derived from Latin word 'persona' meaning 'the mask'. In ancient Greece, the actors used to wear masks to hide their identities while portraying their roles in a theatrical play.

To an ordinary person, the word 'personality' conveys the meaning of one's physical appearance, his habits, his ways of dressing, his reputation, his manners and other similar characteristics.

Sports plays an important role in developing the personality in the following ways

(i) **Development of Physique** A good physique can be developed by regular training which becomes simple by participation in sports. A well-built physique exhibits good personality that is attractive and impressive.

(ii) **Relieve Stress** Stress can be relieved by playing any type of sport. Sports help one combat anxiety, depression and stress. When the stress is relieved from the person, it improves the personality of that person.

(iii) **Social Skills** Sports help in developing social skills as players play together. bond with each other, share their problems and worries as well as cooperate with each other.

(iv) **Discipline** Sports help in making a person disciplined as it is essential to practise, complete all the tasks on time without fear of failure. This helps in making of a good personality.

2. What is personality trait? Explain about the related theory in detail.

Or Elaborate any three components of Big Five Theory of personality.

(CBSE 2020)

Ans. Personality trait refers to the quality or characteristics that describe a personality. In order to classify different personalities, they are divided into five parts which is known as the big five personality model.

Each part of the model describes a personality trait which is as follows

(i) **Openness** It refers to how a person is inclined to face cultural norms. Its characteristics are imagination, insight. creativity, adventurous and abstract thinking. They are open to change.

(ii) **Conscientiousness** It refers to dutiful and disciplined life. The characteristics include high level of thoughtfulness, good impulse control, goal directed behaviours and risk taking ability.

(iii) **Extroversion** It refers to the type of emotional expression and attitude. Its characteristics include socialability, talkative and assertiveness. It shows how social a person is, or how loving, caring and warm.

(iv) **Agreeableness** It refers to the attributes like cooperation, kindness, trust, affection and other social behaviours. It also shows being dependable, trustworthy and caring personality.

(v) **Neuroticism** It refers to nervousness, worrying nature and anxiety. The characteristics are sadness, moodiness, emotional instability and irritability.

3. Discuss about the psychological benefits of exercise in detail.

Ans. The psychological benefits of exercise are as follows

(i) **Enhances Mood** Exercise increases the supply of certain neurotransmitters in the brain that keep one happy as well as boosting endorphins which are 'feel-good' chemicals. These chemicals help in uplifting the mood, thereby reducing depression.

(ii) **Reduces Anxiety and Stress** Exercise is correlated to a reduction in anxiety as exercise stimulates anti-anxiety effect. It removes the build up of stress hormones in the body. Exercise also improves sleep which helps in reducing stress.

(iii) **Improves Self-Esteem** Exercise has a positive influence on our perception of ourselves, providing a sense of accomplishment as we master skills, improve our body image and self-worth. It is a part of positive coping strategy.

(iv) **Emotional Control** Exercise helps to control various emotions such as depression, anger and anxiety. It also helps to channelise the emotions in a positive way. This helps in the overall development of an individual.

(v) **Keep Mentally Fit** Regular exercise prevents degenerative diseases that occur with age. This prevents cognitive decline by keeping the brain healthy. As a result, a person doing regular exercises is mentally fit.

4. What are the reasons behind doing exercises?

Ans. The main reasons behind doing exercises are as follows

(i) **Longevity** People who are physically active live longer. Regular exercise habit reduces the risk of dying prematurely.

(ii) **Weight Control** Regular physical activity helps to reach and maintain a healthy weight. Exercises speed up the rate of energy usage, resulting in increased metabolism. When metabolism increases, the body weight remains under-control.

(iii) **Bone Strength** An active lifestyle benefits bone density. Regular weight-bearing exercise promotes bone formation, delays bone loss and protect against osteoporosis (form of bone loss associated with aging).

(iv) **Strong Immune System** Regular exercise is beneficial for immune system. Exercise or physical activity may help flush bacteria out of the lungs and airways.

This increases the immunity of body and reduces chance of getting a cold, flu or other illness.

(v) **Cholesterol Lowering Effect** Physical exercise favourably influences blood cholesterol levels in our body. Exercise positively alters cholesterol metabolism by increasing the production and action of several enzymes in the body.

(vi) **Improves Psychological Health** Exercise plays a vital role in improving and maintaining our psychological or emotional health as it releases chemicals like endorphins into our brain which makes us feel happier.

It also helps in combatting the problems of anxiety, depression and stress. It can help in improving self-esteem and self-confidence of an individual.

(vii) **Enhanced Physical Appearance** Exercise can enhance our physical appearance and helps us to maintain a healthy physical appearance for a healthy life.

• Case Based Questions

1. Carl Lewis is a renowned long jumper. Whenever he is going to jump in a competition, he asks the audience to clap their hands till the completion of his jump. **(CBSC Question Bank 2021)**

(i) What do you understand by motivation?

Ans. Motivation means an inspiration, an inner urge to do something or to achieve a target or a goal.

(ii) How many types of motivation are there?

Ans. There are two types of motivation. These are intrinsic and extrinsic. Intrinsic means internally motivated and extrinsic means motivation from outside.

2. Vijay is a football player of Kennedy School. He is famous for his aggressive play in the field. Because of his aggression he scored many goals. At the same time, he was punished for his aggressive behaviour with opponent.

(i) In what ways players show aggressive behaviour?

Ans. Players show aggressive behaviour by hitting or using abusive language. They may also push, insult or threat other players.

(ii) What kind of aggression is shown by Vijay?

Ans. The kind of aggression shown by Vijay is hostile aggression. He may have insulted, hurt, used abusive languages against other players and he was punished for the same.

3. The knowledge of psychology helps the physical educators and the coaches to understand the behaviour of players and how desirable changes and modifications can be brought in their behavioural pattern to improve the level of their performance. Based on this passage, answer the questions.

(i) What is sports psychology?

Ans. It is the branch of psychology that deals with the study of human behaviour on the play field, both under practice and in competitive situations, to bring out qualitative improvement.

(ii) Which psychological factors affect the performance of players?

Ans. Factors like interest, attitude, emotion, stress, motivation, aggression, jealousy, anxiety, etc, affect the performance of players.

Chapter Test

Multiple Choice Questions

1. ______ means the individual's motivational stimuli are coming from within.
   - (a) Internal or Intrinsic motivation
   - (b) External or Extrinsic motivation
   - (c) Psychological motivation
   - (d) Extreme motivation

2. Which sports are most suitable for Endomorphs?
   - (a) Swimming and Basketball
   - (b) Weight-lifting and Power-lifting
   - (c) Cricket and Football
   - (d) None of these

3. ______ have a rectangular shaped body with athletic physique and a balanced body composition.
   - (a) Endomarphs
   - (b) Echomorphs
   - (c) Mesomorphs
   - (d) Extroverts

4. Find the incorrect statement.
   - (a) Ectomorph have less muscle mass and elongated limbs.
   - (b) Openness is characterised by imagination and insight.
   - (c) Conscientiousness include high level of thoughtfulness.
   - (d) Extroversion means energetic but mostly confined to internal world.

5. Find the odd one out.
   - (a) Goal
   - (b) Reward
   - (c) Punishment
   - (d) Spectators

Short Answer (SA) Type Questions

7. Explain how competition and spectators provide motivation?

8. Explain the attribute of thinking-feeling and Judging-Perceiving.

9. List and explain any three concepts of OCEAN.

10. Explain the importance of motivation in sports.

11. What do you understand by hostile aggression? Explain with an example.

Long Answer (LA) Type Questions

12. What is aggression? How aggression affects sports performances?

13. Explain how internal, external motivation, active participation, evaluations and equipments help to motivate people specially players.

Answers

1. (a)   *2.* (b)   *3.* (c)   *4.* (d)   *5.* (a)

CHAPTER 05

Training in Sports

In this Chapter...

- Strength
- Endurance
- Speed
- Flexibility
- Coordinative Abilities

The term 'training' refers to an organised and systematic instructional process which aims at improving an individual's ability to accomplish his assigned roles effectively and meaningfully. However, this kind of understanding of the term training cannot be applied to the concept of sports training.

The term 'sports training' is specifically used in the context of athletics, sports and games which could be a training of sportspersons, coaches and teachers of physical education.

Sports training is a special process of participation of sportspersons based on scientific principles, aimed at improving and maintaining higher performance capacity in different sports activities.

It is a particular type of training designed to improve fitness and abilities to perform in a given sports. It includes **strength, endurance, speed, flexibility, cardiovascular training,** etc. It also includes mental and psychological training and advises on nutritional values.

Strength

Strength is an essential component of physical fitness. It means the capacity to withstand force or pressure. Strength refers to the ability of a muscle to exert force or overcome resistance. Strength in sports refers to muscular strength.

For a sportsperson, strength is very essential as it is required to carry out the physical activities in an effective manner.

According to **Brian Mac**, "Strength is the ability to exert force against a resistance."

According to **Barrow** and **McGee**, "Strength is the capacity of the whole body or of any of its parts to exert force."

Types of Strength

Strength can be divided into the following types

Dynamic Strength

This strength is also known as **isotonic strength**, as it is related to movements. It is the strength in which an individual needs to sustain his body over a prolonged period of time or to be able to apply some force against an object.

For example, a gymnast needs dynamic strength to complete the routine. Other examples are wrestling, rowing or in your daily life, going up stairs or lifting objects, bags, boxes, etc.

It can be further divided into three types, which are as follows

1. **Maximum Strength** It refers to the greatest force that is possible in one single effort. It is basically the ability of muscles to overcome against maximum resistance.

It is used in those sports where players have to tackle maximum resistance like weightlifting, shot put, hammer throw etc. It is also required in sports where maximum strength is needed for start like gymnastics.

2. **Explosive Strength** It refers to the ability to apply strength along with high speed. In other words, it is the ability to overcome resistance with high speed.

   It is required in long jump, high jump, sprints as well as all throwing events. It is also used for jumping in basketball and volleyball.

3. **Strength Endurance** It refers to the ability of the muscles to overcome resistance even under conditions of fatigue. It is a combination of strength and endurance abilities.

   It is used in long distance races, swimming, cycling, pole vault, judo because players have to carry on for a long time period.

Static Strength

This strength is also known as **isometric strength**. It is the ability of muscles to act against resistance from one position.

In other words, it is the greatest amount of strength that can be applied to an immovable object. It is the ability to apply a force where the length of the muscle does not change and there is no visible movement at a joint.

For example, you need static strength to maintain a posture or push a heavy object. In sports, weightlifting is a good example.

Training Methods for Improving Strength

There are three different methods of training to develop or improve strength. These are discussed as follows

Isometric Exercises

These exercises were introduced by **Hettinger** and **Muller** in 1953. The word 'isometric' is derived from the words 'iso' meaning 'same' and '*metric*' meaning 'length'. Thus, the word isometric refers to the length of the muscle that remains unchanged during workouts.

This happens when there is a tension on a muscle but no movement is made, causing the length of the muscle to remain the same. Therefore, one cannot see any external movement but a muscle is stretched as a lot of pressure is exerted on it.

These exercises are very helpful in sports like archery, yoga, judo, weightlifting etc. Examples of these exercises are pressing or pushing a wall, lifting a very heavy weight, pulling the rope in tug-of-war, etc.

Holding Dumbbell Side Ways

Holding Legs at 45°

Examples of Isometric Exercises

Method of Doing Isometric Exercise

These exercises can be done with or without using equipments.

1. **Isometric with Equipment** Doing exercises with equipment requires a bench, a bar, power rack and weights of different sizes. For doing bench press, adjust the power rack by setting the pins at the appropriate height. Load the bar with weights and start pushing the bar upwards.

2. **Isometric without Equipment** Squat, lunge, push-ups are some isometric exercises that can be done without using any equipment.

   For doing push-ups, lay your palms flat on the floor and with the help of feet and hands, lift your body upwards. Then, hold in that position for 20 seconds and release your weight by coming back to the original position.

Isotonic Exercises

These exercises were developed by **De Loone** in 1954. The word 'isotonic' is derived from Latin words '*iso*' meaning 'same' and '*tonic*' meaning 'muscle tone'. Thus, the word isotonic refers to the toning of the muscles by repetitive exercises. Here, external movement in the muscles can be seen clearly.

When the muscles contract repeatedly, then they develop strength and endurance. The muscle or group of muscles changes in size, *i.e.* shortens and lengthens during action.

Isotonic exercises are of two types. These are as follows

- **Concentric** It means upward movement of the muscles like lifting dumbbells, throwing a ball etc. It shortens the muscles as person overcome the force of a weight.
- **Eccentric** It means downward movement of the muscles like lowering the dumbbells down. It lengthens the muscles while being opposed by the force of a weight.

Method of Doing Isotonic Exercises

For performing squats with weights, make sure your knees are in line with feet. Then, pull the weight by using abs, back and hip muscles. Keep your weight distributed throughout your feet and pull the weight upto shoulder level.

Squat Workout

Lifting weights, arm curling, wrist curling are some of the isotonic exercises. When users workout with much heavier weights, it causes a specific increase in muscle size, because the high weight load leads to tiny tears in the muscle tissue. This causes enlarging of the muscle when they are repaired by the body.

Arm Curling Exercise

Isokinetic Exercises

These exercises were developed by **Perrine** in 1968. The word 'isokinetic' is made from words '*iso*' meaning 'same' and '*kinetic*' meaning 'motion'.

Therefore, isokinetic exercises refers to the exercises that are based on the movement of the muscles throughout the range of the joint with a constant speed.

Examples of isokinetic exercises are pedalling cycle and arm stroke in swimming. In **cycling**, the muscles around the knees move around the entire joint and in **swimming**, there is complete movement of the muscles around the shoulder joint.

Method of Doing Isokinetic Exercises

Start by doing the isokinetic exercises slowly, so that there is no unnecessary pressure. Then, slowly increase the speed and velocity of the exercises allowing for more controlled muscle development and muscle flexibility. For example, to exercise cycling, start with a slow speed of 10-20 kmph and gradually increase it.

Endurance

Endurance is the ability to do sports movement with the desired quality and speed under the conditions of fatigue.

According to **Harre** (1986), "Endurance is the ability to resist fatigue." It is measured by the duration of an activity or how long an exercise can be continued.

Types of Endurance

The types of endurance can be divided on the basis of nature and duration of activity.

On the Basis of Nature of Activity

According to the nature of activity, the endurance is classified into the following types

1. **Basic Endurance** Basic endurance is the ability to perform movements in which large number of body muscles are involved and the activity is performed at slow speed or pace for a long duration such as walking, jogging, slow running, etc. It is also known as aerobic endurance.

2. **General Endurance** It means the ability of body to tolerate fatigue satisfactorily caused by different types of activities. It is not specific to any sports, whereas, it is developed through general exercises. If the general endurance is better, than the performance in sports will also be better.

3. **Specific Endurance** It is the ability to resist the fatigue caused by a particular sports activity. The nature of fatigue and specific endurance is different from sports to sports.

On the Basis of Duration of Activity

According to the duration of the activity, the endurance is classified into following types

1. **Speed Endurance** It is the ability to resist fatigue in activities that last upto 45 seconds. For example, 400 m sprint race. Speed endurance is mainly dependent on the power and capacity of energy production.

2. **Short-term Endurance** It is the ability to resist fatigue in activities that range from 45 seconds to 2 minutes. For example, 800 m race. This endurance depends on strength and speed endurance.

3. **Medium-term Endurance** It is the ability to resist fatigue in activities that range from 2 minutes to 11 minutes. For example, 1500 m race. This endurance also depends on strength and speed endurance, but upto a limited degree.

4. **Long-term Endurance** It is the ability to resist fatigue in activities that last more than 11 minutes. For example, marathon, that requires such type of endurance.

Training Methods for Endurance Development

Training methods for endurance development are as follows

Continuous Training

This method was developed by **Dr Van Aaken**. Continuous training involves continuous running activity or exercise without rest or pause. It allows the body to work from its aerobic energy stores to improve overall fitness and endurance.

Benefits of continuous training includes fat burning, muscle building, and increasing maximum aerobic potential.

For example, long distance running at a stretch. It is divided into three parts

1. **Slow Continuous Method** In this method, the intensity of exercise is low and heart rate remains stable. This means a 10 kilometre run with a heart beat of 140-160 beats per minute. This method is effective for long cross country runs.

2. **Fast Continuous Method** In this method, the intensity is high, heart rate is high and duration is less. The heart beat reaches to 160-180 beats per minute due to increase in intensity. It is for well trained athletes who can run without any pause. It is very effective for improving the VO_2 capacity.

3. **Variable Pace Method** This is a combination of slow and fast continuous method therefore the intensity varies. The heart beat varies under 140-180 beats and time is 15-60 minutes.

   This method is effective for players of almost all games and sports. This includes cycling and jogging.

Advantages

- It increases the efficiency of heart and lungs.
- It also increases muscle mass and endurance.
- Heavy equipments are not required for training.
- It helps an individual to be self-disciplined and self-confident.

Disadvantages

- It does not improve anaerobic fitness.
- It can be hard to keep going when you start to fatigue.

Interval Training

This method was given by **Woldemar** and **Greshler** in 1939. Physiologist Reindell further modified this training method.

This method enhances speed and endurance ability. In this method, the exercises are followed by a period of rest, also known as recovery.

Under this method of training, recovery period is given to an athlete after each speedy workout and it can be adjusted according to the efficiency of athlete.

Interval Training Method

This method mainly trains the heart. This is done by following a pattern of exercises like slow and fast exercises along with a period of recovery.

For example,

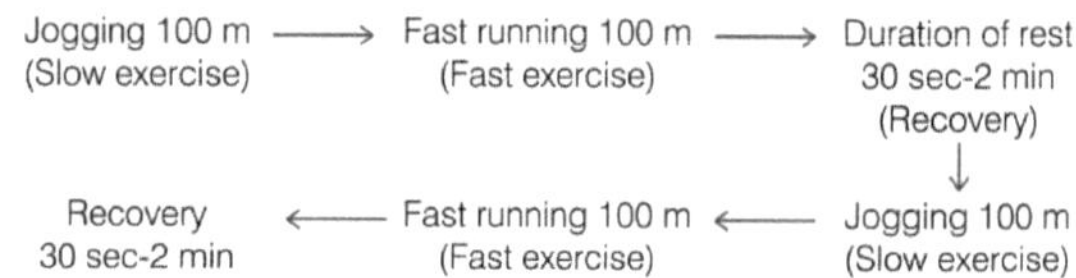

Following factors are essential to note down

- Distance of exercise
- Speed/Intensity
- Duration of work and rest
- Frequency/Number of repetitions
- Heart rate

According to the above example, noting down the factors will give the following result

- Distance of exercise (run) — 400 m
- Time /duration — 5 minutes (3.5 minutes of run +1.5 minutes of rest)
- Speed — 10-20 kmph in jogging 25-30 kmph in running
- Frequency/repetitions — Any number of repetitions are allowed
- Heart rate — 70-140 beats per minute in jogging 180-200 beats per minute in running

Advantages

- More workout can be performed in short duration.
- It is beneficial for respiratory and circulatory systems.
- The progress can be measured easily.
- An athlete achieves peak performance in short period.

Disadvantages

- There are chances of injury.
- It can lead to heart diseases.

Fartlek Training

This method was introduced by **O Astrand** and **Gosta Halner**. It is good for aerobic and anaerobic fitness.

Fartlek is a Swedish term which means, 'speed play' and has been used by distance runners for years.

Fartlek is a form of road running or cross-country running in which the runner usually changes the pace significantly during the run.

It is a combination of slow and fast running on different terrains, covering hills etc. Self-discipline plays a vital role in this method of training.

Fartlek Training Method

The duration of this training method lasts for 45 minutes or more. It can vary from aerobic walking to anaerobic sprinting. Proper warm up and cooling down is required to get best results.

This is followed by a vigorous activity like climbing uphill. Then, it is followed by recovery phase where the pace slows down. Again, it is followed by a vigorous activity that needs a lot of effort.

Advantages

- It improves cardiovascular endurance.
- Good for aerobic and anaerobic fitness.
- It makes the body versatile.
- It is flexible in nature.
- It can be adopted easily by the athletes.

Disadvantages

- Difficult to judge the exact efforts of the athletes.
- It may cause accidents.

Speed

It is the ability to cover distance in minimum possible time such as covering a distance in shortest time. In simple words, it means capacity of a moving body part or the whole body with greatest possible velocity.

In other words, it is the ability to do work faster.

According to **Barrow** and **McGee**, "Speed is the capacity of an individual to perform successive movement of the same pattern at a fast rate."

According to **Johnson** and **Nelson,** speed is defined as "the rate at which a person can propel his body, or parts of his body through space."

Types of Speed

In general, speed has several different forms which are seen in most sports movements. These are discussed as follows

1. Reaction Speed

It is the ability to respond to a given stimulus as quickly as possible, like good speed in sprints, speed in fielding, chasing the ball, etc. It is of two types *viz.* simple and complex reaction speed.

- **Simple reaction** speed means reaction to known signals like gun shot at the start of the sprint race.
- **Complex reaction** speed means reaction to unknown signals like facing a ball in cricket.

2. Movement Speed

It is the ability to do a single movement in the minimum time like jumping, throwing, kicking, boxing, gymnastics where movements with speed are necessary. It depends upon techniques, explosive strength, flexibility and coordinative abilities.

3. Acceleration Speed

It is the ability to achieve maximum speed in shortest possible time. This form of speed depends upon explosive strength, frequency of movement and technique. This ability is important in swimming, hockey, football, gymnastics etc.

Training Methods for Speed Development

A speed development programme can be framed according to need, level and training state of the players.

Following are the training methods to develop speed

Acceleration Run

It is generally used to develop speed indirectly by improving explosive strength, technique, flexibility and movement frequency. It is basically the capacity to attain maximum speed in minimum time.

Before acceleration runs, proper warm-up must be done. After every acceleration run, there should be a proper interval so that the athlete may start the next run without any fatigue.

Acceleration Run Method

For acceleration run, sprinter is required to run a specific distance. He starts from stationary position and tries to attain the maximum speed as soon as possible and tries to finish the distance at that speed.

These accelerations are repeated 6 to 12 times with sufficient intervals between runs. The maximum speed should be achieved within 5-6 seconds after the stationary position.

The number of acceleration runs can be fixed according to the age, experience and capacity of the athlete. Thus, it is the ability of the sprinter to achieve high speed from a stationary position.

Pace Run

Pace run means running the whole distance of a race at a constant speed or with uniform speed. Generally, 800 m and above races are included in pace races.

It develops explosive strength and endurance as the athletes run long distances without getting fatigue. Repetitions can be fixed according to the standard of the athletes.

Pace Run Method

This method is useful for longer races. Under this method, the runner conserves his/her energy by reducing the speed.

For example, if there is a runner of 900 m race and his best time is 1 minute 50 seconds, so he should run the first 450 m in 54 seconds and the next 450 m in 56 seconds. This procedure is basically known as pace run.

Flexibility

It means the ability of a joint to perform actions through a range of movements. It is needed to perform everyday activities with relative ease.

Flexibility is affected by the length of the muscle, joint structure, ligaments, tendons and other factors. Flexibility tends to deteriorate with age.

According to **David R Lamb**, "Flexibility is the range of motion of the body's joint."

Types of Flexibility

Flexibility can be divided into two types, which are as follows

1. Passive Flexibility

It is the ability to perform movement with greater range using external help, *i.e.* with the help of an equipment or a partner. For example, using exercise cycle to improve flexibility of lower body.

2. Active Flexibility

It is the ability to perform movement with greater range without using external help, *i.e.* with the help of muscular force. For example, performance of stretching, push-ups, running and other exercises that stretch the muscles of the body.

Active flexibility can be further divided into two types, which are as follows

- **Static Flexibility** It is required by a sportsperson when he remains in a static position, like diving, sitting etc.
- **Dynamic Flexibility** It is required or needed for doing movements with greater distance, when an individual is in motion, like walking, running, etc.

Training Methods to Improve Flexibility

The ways to improve flexibility are as follows

Dynamic Stretching

It refers to stretching that involves putting muscular effort along with movement at the same time. Walking lunges, kicking action, moving the arm in circular motion are examples of dynamic stretching.

Proper warm-up is necessary for these exercises. Speed, muscular effort, movement and rhythm are required in this method.

Dynamic Stretching

Static Active Stretching

Under this method, the muscles are stretched without moving the limbs and the limbs are held in a position for 30 seconds. Standing on one leg and holding the other leg directly in front for 20-30 seconds is static active stretching.

This exercise consists of 1-2 stretches per muscle group for 30 seconds each. It is a warm-up exercise also.

Static Passive Stretching

This also refers to stretching of muscles without moving the limbs. However, an external force is applied to hold the stretch in position.

The external force can be some other part of your body like hands to hold the stretch, an assistance or an equipment.

For example, bringing your leg up high and then holding it there with your hand. It is also a warm up exercise and a form of isometric exercise.

Static Passive Stretching

Ballistic Stretching

It uses the momentum of a moving body or a limb in an attempt to force it beyond its normal range of motion.

This is a stretching or warming up, by bouncing into a stretched position, using the stretched muscles as a spring which pulls you out of the stretched position.

The stretching can be performed rhythmically with a count. At each count, joint is stretched to the maximum limit and then it is again flexed.

This type of stretching can lead to injury, if body is not warmed up. It should proceed from slow swinging exercises in beginning followed by fast swinging exercises.

Ballistic Stretching

PNF Stretching

It refers to Proprioceptive Neuro Muscular Facilitation Technique. This is an advanced technique for improving flexibility. PNF involves both stretching and contraction of specific muscle group. This is done with the help of a partner.

PNF Stretching

The procedure is as follows

- The muscle group to be stretched is positioned and stretched.
- The athlete then contracts the stretched muscle group for 8-10 seconds while a partner applies force to resist the movement.
- An immovable object such as a wall or a heavy equipment can also be used for resistance.
- The contracted muscle group is then relaxed and very little stretch is applied for 20-30 seconds.
- The muscle group is then allowed 30 seconds to recover.
- This process is repeated 3-4 times.

Coordinative Abilities

The term 'coordinative ability' replaced the term 'agility'. The term 'agility' was discarded as it was not clearly defined and there was no unanimity in its meaning.

Coordinative ability mainly depends on the central nervous system. It is the ability to perform smooth and accurate movements involving different parts of the body.

It requires good integration between the senses and muscles as well as good neuromuscular coordination.

In other words, the ability to control the movements of different parts of our body, so that they work well together is called coordinative ability.

Coordinative abilities are essential in sports and games. Infact, the accuracy of actions, rhythm, change of movement, balance, graceful action, etc. all are a product of well-developed technical skills and coordinative abilities.

For example, hockey requires the coordination of hands, eyes and hockey stick as well as good neuromuscular coordination to connect with the ball.

Types of Coordinative Abilities

Different types of coordinative abilities are as follows

Differentiation Ability

It is the ability to achieve a high level of fine tuning of individual movements and body part movements. Highly skilful movements with hand, feet or head increase differentiation ability.

Orientation Ability

It is the ability to determine and change the position and movements of the body in different types of situations. For example, in gymnastics, the position and movement of head and eyes is important for orientation.

Coupling Ability

It is the ability to coordinate body parts movement (For example, movements of hands, feet, trunk etc.) with one another. It is especially important in sports in which fast movements have to be done. For example, gymnastics, team games etc.

Reaction Ability

It is the ability to react quickly and effectively to a signal. There are generally two types of reaction ability, which are as follows

- **Simple reaction** ability is to react immediately to a well-known signal. Here, the signal is known so the reaction is prepared.
- **Complex reaction** ability is the ability to react immediately or quickly to unexpected signals. For example, a batsman facing ball in cricket. Here the signal is unknown so the reaction is spontaneous.

Balance Ability

It is the ability of a sportsperson to maintain equilibrium of the body both in static and dynamic conditions.

In other words, it is the ability to maintain balance during the complete body movements and to regain balance quickly after the balance disturbing movements. This ability is essential in most of the sports and games.

Rhythm Ability

It is the ability to do body movements according to a given rhythm like in gymnastics, performing floor exercises with a definite rhythm. Examples of this type are found in gymnastics, synchronised swimming, diving, skating, etc.

Adaptation Ability

It is the ability to adjust or completely change the movement according to changing situation. It depends on the speed and accuracy with which a situation is adapted. The perfection of this ability is achieved through the mastery of the skills.

Chapter Practice

Objective Questions

• Multiple Choice Questions

1. The ability which help to overcome the resistance with speed, is known as ______.
   (a) Maximum Strength   (b) Explosive Strength
   (c) Static Strength   (d) None of these

Ans. (b) The ability which help to overcome the resistance with high speed is known as explosive strength. It is required in long jump, high jump sprints etc.

2. The method in which there will be no change in the length of the muscle is known as ______.
   (a) Isometric Method
   (b) Isotonic Method
   (c) Isokinetic Method
   (d) Fartlek Method

Ans. (a) The method in which there will be no change in the length of muscles is known as isometric exercises.

3. Which exercise method was developed by De Loone in 1954?
   (a) Isometric Exercises   (b) Isotonic Exercises
   (c) Isokinetic Exercises   (d) None of these

Ans. (b) De Loone in 1954, developed Isotonic exercises which refers to the toning of the muscles by doing repetitive exercises.

4. While exercising on a multigym, the type of muscular contraction that occurs is   **(CBSE 2020)**
   (a) Isotonic   (b) Isometric
   (c) Isokinetic   (d) Eccentric

Ans. (b) While exercising on a multigym, the muscular contraction occurs is isometric. Here the length of the muscle remains unchanged but a tension on the muscle causes it to strengthen.

5. Resistance ability against fatigue is called
   (CBSE 2020)
   (a) Strength   (b) Speed
   (c) Endurance   (d) Agility

Ans. (c) Resistance ability against fatigue is called endurance.

6. Identify the kind of strength training exercise shown in the picture.

   (a) Isometric   (b) Isotonic   (c) Isokinetic   (d) Ballistic

Ans. (b) The kind of strength training workout shown in the image is squat workout. This is isotonic as there is repetitive workout of muscle toning.

7. The exercise shown below enhances which component of physical fitness?

   (a) Flexibility   (b) Speed   (c) Strength   (d) Endurance

Ans. (a) The exercise Ballistic stretching enhances flexibility. Here force is applied on a limb in an attempt to force it beyond its normal range of motion.

8. Match the following.

List I (Type of Endurance)	List II (Examples)
A. Short-term Endurance	1. Marathon
B. Speed Endurance	2. 400 m Sprint race
C. Medium-term Endurance	3. 800 m race
D. Long-term Endurance	4. 1500 m race

Codes

	A	B	C	D			A	B	C	D
(a)	3	2	4	1		(b)	3	4	2	1
(c)	4	3	1	2		(d)	1	2	3	4

Ans. (a) The correct answer is A-3, B-2, C-4, D-1.

9. Match the following.

	List I		List II
A.	PNF Stretching	1.	Kicking action in a circular motion.
B.	Dynamic Stretching	2.	Bringing your leg up high and then holding it there with your hand.
C.	Static Active Stretching	3.	Muscles are stretched without moving the limbs.
D.	Static Passive Stretching	4.	Involves both stretching and contraction of specific muscle group.

Codes

	A	B	C	D			A	B	C	D
(a)	4	3	2	1		(b)	4	1	3	2
(c)	1	2	3	4		(d)	3	4	2	1

Ans. (b) The correct match is A-4, B-1, C-3, D-2.

10. Which type of exercise are being explained by the sports instructor?
(a) Isotomic
(b) Isokinetic
(c) Isometric
(d) Pace run

Ans. (b) Isokinetic type of exercise are being explained by sports instructor. In isokinetic exercises there is complete movement of the muscles throughout the range of joint with a constant speed.

11. Strength is the capacity of the whole body or any of its parts to exert force. Strength is divided into dynamic strength and static strength. Dynamic strength is again divided into maximum strength, explosive strength and strength endurance.

In the sport shown below, which type of strength is used?

(a) Explosive strength
(b) Static strength
(c) Maximum strength
(d) Both (b) and (c)

Ans. (d) In the sport of weightlifting, static strength and maximum strength are used. Static is the ability of muscles to resist and maximum strength is the greatest force possible in one single effort.

12. Sunita, a student of class VIII, was identified as a strong girl both physically and mentally. She is being encouraged by her teacher to take up wrestling as a professional sport and start training. She expresses her interest to her family that she wants to learn boxing but her brothers made fun of her and ridiculed her. Her father on seeing her interest sent her to a professional coach to learn that sport properly.

Which component of physical fitness is most important for a sport like wrestling?
(a) Speed
(b) Strength
(c) Endurance
(d) Flexibility

Ans. (b) Strength is the most important conponent of physical fitness that is required in wrestling. It means the capacity to withstand force or pressure.

13. Raman practices pace run technique to increase his speed as he wants to take part in the Athletics meet to be held in his school next month.

Generally what is the length of Pace run?
(a) 100 m
(b) 200 m
(c) 400 m
(d) 800 m

Ans. (d) Pace run usually consist of 800 m running. It means running the whole distance of a race at a constant speed.

14. In sports, different types of coordinative abilities are needed. These abilities depend on the central nervous system.

Which ability determines and changes the position and movements of the body in different types of situations?
(a) Balance Ability
(b) Orientation Ability
(c) Rhythm Ability
(d) Adaptation Ability

Ans. (b) Orientation ability is the ability to determine and change the position and movements of a body in different situations in gymnastic. Here position and movement of eyes and head is important.

15. Ravi has the aim of joining any of the uniform services like police, army, air force etc. But he has not qualified the 1500 m run in their selection criteria. Without qualifying this run, he can't go for the next level.

1500 m run is conducted to find the
(a) Endurance ability
(b) Speed
(c) Strength
(d) Explosive

Ans. (a) 1500 m run is conducted to find the endurance ability which is the ability of the body to do movements even under conditions of fatigue.

• Assertion-Reasoning MCQs

Directions (Q. Nos. 1-4) *Each of these questions contains two statements, Assertion (A) and Reason (R). Each of these questions also has four alternative choices, any one of which is the correct answer. You have to select one of the codes (a), (b), (c) and (d) given below.*

Codes

(a) Both A and R are true and R is the correct explanation of A

(b) Both A and R are true, but R is not the correct explanation of A

(c) A is true, but R is false

(d) A is false, but R is true

1. Assertion (A) Coordinative ability mainly depends on the central nervous system.

Reason (R) It needs good integration between the senses and muscles as well as good neuromuscular coordination.

Ans. (a) The assertion is true as the nervous system manages the coordinative abilities of our body. Balance, control, coordination, orientation rhythm all depends on it. Reason is also true proper integration is needed for good neuromuscular coordination. Thus, Both A and R are true and R is the correct explanation of A.

2. Assertion (A) Sports movements continued with quality and speed is endurance.

Reason (R) It is the ability of the muscles to overcome resistance over longer duration of exercises or physical essertion.

Ans. (a) Assertion is true as endurance is to continue an activity by resisting fatigue. So it is a combination of speed and quality. Reason is also correct as strength means to overcome resistance and endurance means to continue that for longer duration. So reason explains assertion. Thus, both A and R are true and R is the correct explanation of A.

3. Assertion (A) Sequential movements performed with smothness and accuracy is flexibility.

Reason (R) Different types of coordinative abilities bring perfection in sports performances.

Ans. (d) Assertion is false as flexibility refers to elasticity and stretchability of the body. Sequential movements can be related to coordinative ability. Reason is true as coordinative abilities are a combination of neuromuscular and sensory ability that bring perfection in our movements. Thus, A is false, but R is true.

4. Assertion (A) High speed of locomotion from a stationary position or slow moving is acceleration run.

Reason (R) The racing ability is improved indirectly by improving on explosive strength and technique.

Ans. (b) Assertion is true acceleration run is part of speed training that may be in high speed or slow speed.

Reason is also true as explosive strength and technique improves the racing ability. But reason do not explains anything about assertion i.e., acceleration run.

Thus, both A and R are true, but R is not the correct explanation of A.

• Case Based MCQs

1. The sports instructor explained the concept of movements of hands and legs in swimming. He told to move the hands completely so the muscles around the shoulder joint also moves fully.

(CBSE Question Bank 2021)

Running　Sprint　Walk
Jogging
Start　Exercises (Few)
Push-ups
Slow Running　Frog jump
Fast Running
Sprint　Hopping
Finish
Running Fast

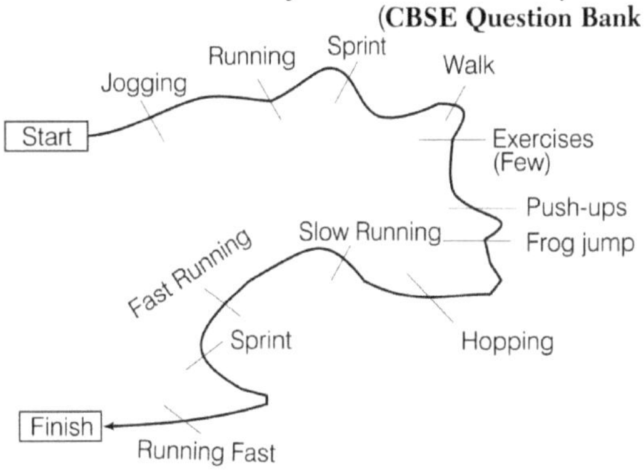

(i) From the above picture, it is identified as .... training method.

(a) Pace runs　(b) Fartlek　　(c) Isometric　(d) Isotonic

Ans. (b) From the above picture, it is identified as Fartlek training method.

(ii) The above training method helps in increasing the ....

(a) strength　　　　　　　(b) speed

(c) endurance　　　　　　(d) flexibility

Ans. (c) The above training method helps in increasing the endurance as it is a combination of vigorous activity followed by recovery and again vigorous.

(iii) The Swedish word meaning 'Speed Play' is

(a) Citius　　　　　　　　(b) Fartlek

(c) Pace　　　　　　　　(d) Altius

Ans. (b) The swedish word meaning 'speed play' is called Fartlek. It was introduced by OA stand and Gosta Halner.

2. Mr. Gopichand is a renowned badminton coach. When he started his academy, he selected our school badminton players and designed a training program. During the training, he noted that few players were good in defense but due to lack of endurance and strength, they were unable to play up to the last moment. He used various methods to enhance their endurance and strength.

(CBSE Question Bank 2021)

(i) This type of training and exercises help in increasing the static strength and maximal strength.

(a) Isometric (b) Isotonic

(c) Isokinetic (d) Aerobic

Ans. (a) Isometric exercises help in increasing the static strength and maximal strength. In this the length of the muscle remains unchanged during workouts.

(ii) Isotonic exercise helps in enhancing

(a) Speed (b) Strength

(c) Agility (d) Endurance

Ans. (b) Isotonic exercises help in enhancing strength by toning of the muscles through repeated exercises.

(iii) High pressure over muscles can be seen in these set of exercises

(a) Isometric

(b) Isotonic

(c) Both (a) and (b)

(d) Ballistic

Ans. (c) High pressure over muscles can be seen in the isometric and isotonic form of exercises. All the workouts are related to muscular movements.

PART 2
Subjective Questions

• Short Answer (SA) Type Questions

1. What is strength? What are the different types of strength?

Ans. Strength is the capacity to withstand force or pressure. It refers to muscular strength. Types of strength are as follows

(i) **Maximum Strength** It refers to the greatest force that is possible in a single maximum muscle contraction or one single effort.

(ii) **Explosive Strength** It refers to the ability to apply strength along with high speed.

(iii) **Strength Endurance** It refers to ability of the muscles to overcome resistance under fatigue.

2. Differentiate between isometric and isotonic exercises. **(CBSE 2020, 2016)**

Ans. The difference between Isometric and Isotonic are as follows

Isometric Exercises	Isotonic Exercises
An isometric exercise occurs when there is tension on a muscle without any movement. The length of the muscles remains same.	Isotonic exercises involve controlled movements of muscles and mobilisation of the joints around those muscles.
Less or no equipment required.	Sometimes equipment is required to perform them.
It needs less time.	The time period is more in comparison.

3. List the advantages and disadvantages of Isometric exercises.

Ans. Advantages of Isometric exercises are as follows

• In isometric exercises, less or no equipments are required as immovable objects are used.

• Less time is required to perform whereas effects are more.

• Isometric strength training exercises develop high level of static strength and maximal strength, thus, effective for total muscular strength.

• These exercises can be performed during warming-up session.

Disadvantages of Isometric exercises are as follows

• Isometric exercise raise the blood pressure.

• It develops static strength whereas in most of the games and sports dynamic strength is required.

• There is less variety of isometric exercises.

4. Isometric exercises are a very important method for developing physical fitness. Describe what do you understand about them.

Ans. Isometric exercises are a type of muscle workout. In this, you perform isometric muscle contraction. It means that the muscle contraction occurs when your muscle exerts force without changing its length, i.e. without movement. In other words, when you do an isometric muscle contraction, your joint doesn't move. Unlike concentric (when the muscle shortens as it works) and eccentric (when the muscle lengthens when it works) types of contractions, isometric muscle contraction neither lengthens nor shortens the muscle fibres but strengthens them.

5. What is endurance? Which method will you suggest to develop endurance?

Ans. Endurance is the ability to do sports movements with the desired quality and speed under the conditions of fatigue. Fartlek training method is essential to develop endurance. Fartlek is a form of road running in which the runner usually changes the pace significantly during the run.

The duration of this training lasts for 45 minutes or more. It is followed by walking to sprinting and from rigorous exercises to recovery phases. It is suited to improve cardiovascular endurance.

6. Explain interval training method.   **(All India 2017)**

Or What is endurance? Explain the various methods of its development.

Ans. Endurance is the ability to do sports movements with the desired quality and speed under conditions of fatigue.

The methods to develop endurance are as follows

(i) **Continuous Training Method** This method was developed by Dr Van Aaken. Continuous training involves continuous running activity or exercise without rest or pause. For example, long distance running at a stretch.

(ii) **Interval Training Method** This method enhances speed and endurance ability. In this method, the exercises are followed by a period of rest, also known as recovery.

7. What is Fartlek training?

Or What does the term Fartlek mean and who developed this training method?   **(All India 2017)**

Ans. Fartlek is a Swedish term which means 'speed play' and has been used by distance runner for years. It improves individual's speed and endurance. It is a form of road running or cross country running in which the runner usually changes the pace significantly during the run.

This method was introduced by O Astrand and Gosta Halner. It is a combination of slow and fast running on different terrains, covering hills etc.

8. Explain the advantages of Fartlek training.

Ans. Advantages of Fartlek training are as follows

- It is good for increasing strength and cardiorespiratory endurance.
- Several athletics can take part in the training programme at a time.
- It does not require any equipment and can be organised easily.
- This training method is not rigid; it is flexible in nature.
- It improves the efficiency of the heart and lungs.

9. Define speed and explain any one method to develop it.   **(CBSE 2020)**

Or Define speed. Explain the methods of speed development.   **(Delhi 2016, 15)**

Ans. It is the ability to cover distance in minimum possible time. It is also the quickness of movement of body parts such as fast skipping, jumping, etc.

Speed Developing Methods

(i) **Acceleration Run** It is usually used to develop speed indirectly by improving explosive strength, technique, flexibility and movement frequency.

Before acceleration runs, proper warm up must be done. After every acceleration run, there should be a proper interval so that the athlete may start the next run without any fatigue.

(ii) **Pace Races** Pace races mean running the whole distance of a race at a constant speed or with uniform speed.

It develops explosive strength and endurance as the athletes run long distances without fatigue. Repetitions can be fixed according to the standard of the athletes.

10. Explain the physiological factors determining speed.

Or Write in brief about any three physiological factors determining speed.   **(Delhi 2016, 14)**

Or Explain the types of speed.   **(All India 2012)**

Ans. The physiological factors determining speed are as follows

(i) **Reaction Speed** It is the ability to respond to a given stimulus as quickly as possible, like good speed in sprints, speed in fielding, chasing the ball etc.

(ii) **Movement Speed** It is the ability to do a single movement in the minimum time like jumping, throwing, kicking, boxing etc.

(iii) **Acceleration Speed** It is the ability to achieve maximum speed in shortest possible time. This form of speed depends upon explosive strength, frequency of movement and technique. This ability is important in swimming, hockey, football, gymnastics etc.

11. What is flexibility? Explain its types.

Ans. Flexibility is the ability of a joint to perform action through a range of movements. It is needed to perform everyday activities with relative ease. Flexibility tends to deteriorate with age.

Flexibility is of two types. These are as follows

(i) **Active** It is the ability to perform movement with greater range without using external help i.e. with the help of muscular force e.g. stretching exercises using push-ups etc.

(ii) **Passive** It is the ability to perform movement with greater range using external help i.e. with the help of an equipment or a partner.

12. Briefly explain any three coordinative abilities.

(All India 2016)

Ans. The different types of coordinative abilities are as follows

  (i) **Differentiation Ability** It is the ability to achieve a high level of fine tuning or harmony of individual movement phases and body part movements.

  (ii) **Orientation Ability** It is the ability to determine and change the position and movements of the body in different types of situations. For example, in gymnastics, the position and movement of head and eyes is important for orientation.

  (iii) **Coupling Ability** It is the ability to coordinate body part movements (e.g. movements of hand, feet, trunk etc) with one another.

  Coupling ability is especially important in sports in which movements with a high degree of difficulty have to be done e.g. gymnastics, team games etc.

• Long Answer (LA) Type Questions

1. Write in detail about strength improving methods Isometric, Isotonic and Isokinetic.   (CBSE 2019)

Ans. There are three different methods of training to develop or improve strength. These are discussed as follows

  (i) **Isometric Exercises** These exercises were introduced by Hettinger and Muller in 1953. This happens when there is a tension on a muscle but no movement is made, causing the length of the muscle to remain the same.

  Therefore, one cannot see any external movement but a muscle is stretched as a lot of pressure is exerted on it.

  These exercises are very helpful in sports like archery, yoga, judo, weightlifting etc. Example of these exercises are pressing or pushing a wall, lifting a very heavy weight, pulling the rope in tug-of-war etc.

  (ii) **Isotonic Exercises** These exercises were developed by De Loone in 1954. Here, external movement in the muscles can be seen clearly.

  When the muscles contract repeatedly, then they develop strength and endurance. The muscles or group of muscles changes in size, i.e. shortens and lengthens during action.

  Isotonic exercises are of two types

  • **Concentric** It means upward movement of the muscles like lifting dumbbells, throwing a wall, etc. It shortens the muscles as you overcome the force of a weight.

  • **Eccentric** It means downward movement of the muscles like lowering the dumbbells down. It lengthens the muscles while being opposed by the force of a weight.

  (iii) **Isokinetic Exercises** These exercises were developed by Perrine in 1968. Isokinetic exercise refers to the exercises that are based on the movement of the muscles throughout the range of the joint with a constant speed.

  Examples of isokinetic exercises are pedalling in cycling and arm stroke in swimming.

2. In the strength training exercise group, explain the benefits and drawbacks of Isotonic exercises.

Ans. Advantages of Isotonic exercises are as follows

  • It develops dynamic strength. This is mostly required games and sports.

  • These exercises develop strength and endurance and both can be developed together.

  • Isotonic exercises improve flexibility, thus, muscle have more contractility.

  • These exercises are used for developing explosive strength along with strength endurance

Disadvantages of Isotonic exercises are as follows

  • Changes of stress and strain injuries.

  • Sometimes equipments are required to perform.

The methods to develop endurance are

  (i) **Continuous Training Method** This method was developed by Dr Van Aaken. Continuous training involves continuous running actively or exercise without rest or pause. For example, long distance running at a stretch.

  (ii) **Interval Training Method** This method enhances speed and endurance ability. In this method, the exercises are followed by a period of rest, also known as recovery.

3. Define Speed. What are the methods for improving speed.

Ans. Speed is the rate of motion or the rate of change of position. It is expressed as distance moved per unit of time. Speed is defined as the ability and capacity of an individual to perform similar movements consecutively at the fastest rate. For example, short distance races like 100 metres and 200 metres.

Methods for improving speed are as follows

  (i) **Acceleration Runs** It is the ability to increase speed from jogging to running and finally sprinting. It depends on explosive strength, frequency of movement and technique. To utter maximum speed from a stationary position, it should be practised after learning the proper technique for it .

  (ii) **Pace Run** A competitive pace race is a timed race in which the objective is not to finish in the least time, but to finish within the prescribed time and in the best physical condition.

In some races, the prescribed time is very narrowly defined and the winner is the competitor who finishes closest to the prescribed time. Complete recovery is ensured between two repetitions. This implies running the whole distance of a race at an almost constant speed.

4. Define flexibility and explain the methods of flexibility development. **(Delhi 2015)**

Ans. Flexibility is the ability of a joint to perform action through a range of movements. It is needed to perform everyday activities with relative ease. Flexibility tends to deteriorate with age. The methods of flexibility development are as follows

(i) **Dynamic Stretching** It refers to stretching that involves putting muscular effort along with movement at the same time. Walking lungs, kicking action, moving the arm in circular motion are examples of dynamic stretching.

(ii) **Static Active Stretching** Here the muscles are stretched without moving the limbs and the limbs are held to the end position for 30 seconds. Standing on one leg and holding the other leg directly in front for 20-30 seconds is static active stretching.

(iii) **Static Passive Stretching** This also refers to stretching of muscles without moving the limbs. However, an external force is applied to hold the stretch in position.

The external force can be some other part of your body like hands to hold the stretch, an assistance or an equipment.

(iv) **Ballistic Stretching** It uses the momentum of a moving body or a limb in an attempt to force it beyond its normal range of motion.

This is a stretching or warming up, by bouncing into a stretched position, using the stretched muscles as a spring which pulls you out of the stretch position.

This type of stretching can lead to injury, if body is not warmed up.

5. Discuss in detail the different types of coordinative ability. **(CBSE 2020)**

Or What do you understand by coordinative ability? Discuss about different types of coordinative abilities. **(CBSE 2019)**

Ans. The term 'coordinative ability' replaced the tem 'agility'. The term 'agility' was discarded as it was not clearly defined and there was no unanimity in its meaning.

Coordinative ability mainly depends on the central nervous system. It is the ability to perform smooth and accurate movements involving different parts of the body.

The different types of coordinative abilities are as follows

(i) **Differentiation Ability** It is the ability to achieve a high level of fine tuning or harmony of individual movement phases and body part movements.

(ii) **Orientation Ability** It is the ability to determine and change the position and movements of body in different types of situations.

(iii) **Coupling Ability** It is the ability to coordinate body parts movements (e.g. movements of hands, feet, trunk, etc.) with one another. It is especially important in sports in which fast movements have to be done. For example, gymnastics, team games, etc.

(iv) **Reaction Ability** It is the ability to react quickly and effectively to a signal.

(v) **Balance Ability** It is the ability of a sportsperson to maintain equilibrium of the body both in static and dynamic conditions.

(vi) **Adaptation Ability** It is the ability to adjust or completely change the movement according to changing situation. It depends on the speed and accuracy with which a situation is adapted. The perfection of this ability is achieved through the mastery of the skills.

• Case Based Questions

1. Sunita, a student of class VIII, was identified as a strong girl both physically and mentally. She is being encouraged by her teacher to take up wrestling as a professional sport and start training. Sunita is also interested in the sport as she has been watching the sport on the TV and she is highly impressed by the Indian women wrestlers. She expresses her interest to her family that she wants to learn boxing but her brothers made fun of her and ridiculed her. Her father on seeing her interest sent her to a professional coach to learn that sport properly.

(i) What is maximum strength?

Ans. Maximum strength refers to the greatest force that is possible in one single effort. It is basically the ability of muscles to overcome against maximum resistance. It is used in weightlifting, shot put, hammer throw etc.

(ii) Which type of training method should be used by Sunita to develop strength?

Ans. Isometric training method should be developed as Sunita needs static strength. Her muscles should act against resistance from the opponent player.

2. Ravi has the aim of joining any of the uniform services like police, army, air force etc.

For this, he is required to develop the endurance. Based on this, answer the following questions

(i) Which factors are essential to note down in interval training method?

Ans. The factors that are essential to note down are distance of exercise, speed, duration of work and rest, frequency and heart rate.

(ii) What is the difference in continuous and interval training method?

Ans. Continuous involves continuous running activity or exercise without rest. Interval involves exercises follows by a period of rest.

3. Raghu was good thrower. When he joined a new training camp, where he observed some athletes were running on uneven surfaces like bushes, rocks, pits etc. He was in dilemma. Then the coach explained about that training in detail.

(i) What is the procedure of Fartlek training?

Ans. It begins with proper warm up, then aerobic walking to aerobic sprinting, climbing uphill followed by recovery phase and finally cooling down.

(ii) How Fartlek training can help Raghu to become an athlete?

Ans. Fartlek training method provides vigorous activities, tough training which develops endurance needed by the athletes.

Chapter Test

Multiple Choice Questions

1. Which is not the training method to develop endurance?
    (a) Continuous Method   (b) Interval Method
    (c) Post Isometric Stretch Method   (d) Fartlek Method

2. 'Speed play' is another name of which method?
    (a) Interval Method   (b) Continuous Method
    (c) Isokinetic Method   (d) Fartlek Method

3. Ability which helps to change on the spot, predecided movement is known as ______.
    (a) Differentiation Ability   (b) Orientation Ability
    (c) Adaptation Ability   (d) Rhythm Ability

4. Find the incorrect option from the following.
    (a) Static strength is needed to move an object.   (b) Dynamic strength can be divided into 3 types.
    (c) Isometric exercises are part of flexibility training   (d) Endurance is the ability to resist fatigue.

5. Mr Sharma is the physical education instructor of a school. He asked his students to do isometric exercises to develop strength. Which of the following is a special feature of isometric exercises.
    (a) Complete movement of muscles   (b) Towing of the muscles
    (c) No equipment is needed   (d) All of these

Short Answer (SA) Type Questions

6. Explain how isometric exercise can be done with and without equipment.

7. Explain the types of Isotonic exercises.

8. Briefly explain what is Ballistic Stretching?

9. Which component of fitness can be measured by continuous training? List the advantages of this exercise.

10. Explain the step by step procedure of doing PNF stretching.

Long Answer (LA) Type Questions

11. Draw an exercise routine to show interval training.

12. Compare the advantages and disadvantages of Interval training and Fartlek training.

Answers

1. (c)   *2.* (d)   *3.* (c)   *4.* (c)   *5.* (c)

CBSE Term II
Physical Education XII

Practice Papers
1-3

Practice Paper 1[*]
(Solved)

General Instructions

- Time : **2 Hours**
- Max. Marks : **35**

1. There are 9 questions in the question paper. All questions are compulsory.
2. Question no. 1 is a Case Based Question, which has five MCQs. Each question carries one mark.
3. Question no. 2-6 are Short Answer Type Questions. Each question carries 3 marks.
4. Question no. 7-9 are Long Answer Type Questions. Each question carries 5 marks.
5. There is no overall choice. However, internal choices have been provided in some questions. Students have to attempt only one of the alternatives in such questions.

** As exact Blue-print and Pattern for CBSE Term II exams is not released yet, so the pattern of this paper is designed by the author on the basis of trend of past CBSE Papers. Students are advised not to consider the pattern of this paper as official. It is just for practice purpose.*

Case Based Questions

1. The class teacher of VII A observed newly joined student Sekhar's behaviour. He is different from other students. He has difficulty in thinking and understanding concepts taught at school. The class teacher called his parents and suggested them to take him to a psychologist. $(1 \times 5 = 5)$

(i) The person with intellectual disability has IQ between.
    (a) 70-75%   (b) 80-85%
    (c) 85-90%   (d) 90-95%

(ii) Generally intellectual disability occurs before the age of
    (a) 18   (b) 12
    (c) 6   (d) 3

(iii) Disability means
    (a) Impairment of cognitive   (b) Problem of illness
    (c) Not able to work   (d) Impairment of brain

(iv) _______ disability is also called as invisible disability.
    (a) Cognitive   (b) Intellectual
    (c) Physical   (d) Mental

(v) Lack of practical skills like activities of daily living, personal care are the symptoms of __________.
    (a) ADHD   (b) SPD
    (c) Physical disability   (d) Intellectual disability

Short Answer Questions
$(3 \times 5 = 15)$

2. Why asanas have become integral part of good lifestyle? (3)

Or Differentiate between cognitive and intellectual disability.

3. Write a brief note on any two determining factor of strength of a body. (3)

4. What do you mean assertive behaviour in sports? (3)

Or Sanjay is facing problem in maintaining regular adherence to exercises. Suggest any three measures for enhancing adherence to exercise.

5. Describe Movement and Acceleration speed. (3)

6. Enlist the disability etiquette guidelines which should be followed by society toward persons with hearing loss.

Or Describe the procedure of Gomukhasana. (3)

Long Answer Questions

$(5 \times 3 = 15)$

7. Explain the procedures, benefits and contraindications of the Matsyasana. (5)

Or Why the cases of obesity are day by day increasing in the society? Also mention its symptoms and ways to cure it.

8. It is said that 'For healthy cardiorespiratory system one should regularly follow well planned exercise routine." Examine. (5)

Or 'Personality is a dynamic concept.' Describe the different types of personalities on the basis of modern day classification.

9. Define endurance along with its types on the basis of duration of activity. Also, write a brief note on the Continuous Training programme for endurance development. (5)

Or In what way a sport person can increase his/her flexibility?

Answers

1. (i) (a) The person with intellectual disability has IQ between 70-75%.

(ii) (a) Generally intellectual disability occurs before the age of 18.

(iii) (a) Disability means impairment of cognitive.

(iv) (a) Cognitive disability is also called as invisible disability.

(v) (b) Lack of practical skills like activities of daily living, personal care are the symptoms of intellectual disability.

2. Asanas have become integral part of good lifestyle because of following reasons

- Asanas play a significant role in making our muscles strong.
- Asanas improve flexibility of body. They enhance bones, cartileges and ligament.
- With the help of asanas joints are able to bear more pressure.
- With the help of asanas, we can improve our immune system.
- Asanas improve blood circulation and stablise blood pressure. Therefore, they reduce risk of cardiac strokes.

- Asanas ensure smooth functioning of the organ systems in our body such as digestive system, cardiovascular system and circulatory system.
- Asanas also help in mental development as they calm the mind, relieve stress and enhance concentration.
- Performing asanas regularly help in curing many diseases and maintain good health, which increase longevity.

Or

Cognitive disability and intellectual disability may seem the same but there are lots of differences between the two which are as follows

Cognitive disability is more related to weaknesses in certain academic skills like in reading, writing or calculations. It is also known as 'learning difficulty'.

1. Intellectual disability is also known as 'learning disability' and described as below average IQ along with lack of skills needed for daily living.

2. Cognitive disability affects only a certain specific part of the mind. The child performs all the other activities properly.

3. Intellectual disability is more severe in nature as the child is not able to perform even the daily activities along with difficulty in learning.

3. The two important factors of determining strength of body are as follows
    (i) **Size of the Muscle** The size of the muscle determines the strength possessed by an individual. It is well-known fact that bigger and larger muscles can produce more force.

    Males have bigger and larger muscles due to which they have more strength than females. The muscle size can be increased with the help of various methods such as weight training, etc., which will also improve the muscular strength.
    (ii) **Body Weight** There is a positive correlation between the body weight and strength. It has been noticed that individuals with heavier body weight are stronger than the individual with the lighter weight. Thus, body weight also determines the strength of an individual.
4. Assertive behaviour is also referred as assertive aggression. It is generally seen as a positive form of aggression. In ground, it simply means to stand up for your values in an unthreatening manner, and involves the use of legitimate physical or verbal force to achieve one's goals.

    For an act to be assertive, it must be goal directed with no specific intention to harm alongwith the use of legitimate force with no rules broken.

    Thus, assertive behaviour should include four components *viz.* it should be goal oriented, should not be intended to harm, should use only to legitimate force and should not break any rule of the sport.

Or

    Sanjay is facing problem in maintaining adherence to exercises then he should follow following steps
    - **Choose Simple Exercise** The person should choose simple exercises in the beginning, such as walking, jogging, yoga, etc. No equipment or excuses are required for these types of exercises. One can adhere to such exercises due to their nature of simplicity.
    - **Suitable Environment** At the time of exercise training programme, suitable environment should be provided. The environment with latest facilities will help to improve adherence to exercise.
    - **Realistic Plan** Planning and goal setting should be realistic in nature. Goal setting should be according to the capability of a person, as proper plan improves the adherence to exercise.
5. The Movement and Acceleration speed are discussed below
    - **Movement Speed** It is the ability to do a single movement in the minimum time like jumping, throwing, kicking, boxing and gymnastics where movements with speed are necessary. It depends upon techniques, explosive strength, flexibility and coordinative abilities.
    - **Acceleration Speed** It is the ability to achieve maximum speed in shortest possible time. This form of speed depends upon explosive strength, frequency of movement and technique. This ability is important in swimming, hockey, football, gymnastics, etc.
6. The disability etiquette guidelines which should be followed by society toward persons with hearing loss are as follows
    - Get the person's attention with a wave of the hand, or a tap on the shoulder.
    - Speak clearly and slowly, but without exaggerating your lip movements or shouting.
    - Many persons with hearing loss read lips. Place yourself facing the light source and keep hands, cigarettes and food away from your mouth while talking, in order to provide a clear view of your face.
    - When an interpreter accompanies a person, direct your remarks to the person rather than to the interpreter.
    - Look directly at the person and speak expressively.
    - Use sign language if you and the person are familiar with it.

Or

The procedure of Gomukhasana are as follows
- This is done in sitting position.
- Sit straight and stretch both legs together in front.
- Fold right leg at the knee and place it on the ground by the side of the left buttock.
- Bringing the left leg from above the right leg, place it on the ground by the side of the right buttock.
- Fold your left arm and place it behind your back. Then, take your right hand over your right shoulder, and stretch it as much as you can until it reaches your left hand.
- After sometime, return to the original position.
- Change the position of the legs *i.e.* by placing the right knee above and the left knee down and repeat this as much as you can.

7. The procedures, benefits and contraindications of the Matsyasana are as follows

Procedures

This asana is done in lying pose.
- Lift your hips and tuck your hands slightly beneath your buttocks, palms facing down. Draw your forearms and elbows in towards your body.
- With inhale, bend your elbows and press firmly on your forearms and elbows to lift your head and upper body away from the floor.
- Firm your shoulder blades into your back and lift your chest higher towards the ceiling, elongate your spine.
- Bring the crown of your head down on the floor, placing a minimal amount of weight on your head.

- Remain here with your knees bent, or, if it feels uncomfortable, extend both legs straight down on the mat in front of you with your muscles strongly engaged.
- Stay in the pose anywhere from 5 to 10 deep breaths.

Benefits

- It stretches the neck muscles and shoulders.
- This pose provides relief from respiratory disorders by encouraging deep breathing, as this pose increases lung capacity to a great extent.
- There is an increased supply of blood to the cervical and thoracic regions of the back that helps tone the parathyroid, pituitary and pineal glands.
- This pose helps to regulate emotions and stress.
- The practice of Matsyasana brings down the tension and the stiffness at the neck and the shoulders.

Contraindications

- Individuals suffering from high or low blood pressure should avoid this posture.
- Women who are pregnant should not attempt this yoga pose.
- Injury in neck or any part of the lower back or middle back can make it difficult to practice this fish pose and hence should be avoided.

Or

Obesity is referred to a medical condition in which excess body fat is accumulated to the extent that it has a negative effect on health.

Generally, people are considered obese when their Body Mass Index (BMI) is more than 30. Body Mass Index is obtained by dividing a person's weight by the square of the person's height.

The cases of obesity are increasing in the society on a fast rate due to following reasons

- Excess consumption of fats, sugar and calorie-rich foods.
- Improper functioning of certain glands such as endocrine gland system.
- Lack of exercises, less physical activities and sedentry lifestyle.
- Poor lifestyle.

Symptoms of Obesity

- Increase in weight constantly.
- Increase in laziness and rise in intake of food.
- Retardness in mental and emotional activities.
- Frustration and depression.

Preventions

- Take food which contain less fat, fibre-rich vegetables and fruits.
- Reduce the consumption of fats, sweets and junk foods.
- Stop addictions of smoking, drinking and other drugs.
- Increase physical activities, doing regular exercises.

8. In order to keep cardiorespiratory system in good condition a person should always follow well planned exercise routine. Doing regular exercise will be beneficial to cardio respiratory system in following ways

- **Increase in Heart Size** Regular exercises develop the muscles of the heart. It increases the size of the heart along with the strengthening of heart.

  Thus, the heart becomes more efficient in doing its job with the capacity to pump more oxygen-rich blood.

- **Decrease in Cholesterol Level** Regular exercise reduces the level of cholesterol in our blood. The level of cholesterol in our blood is directly linked with blood pressure.

  Exercise decreases the level of low-density protein and increases the level of high-density protein.

  It simply means that exercise decreases the LDL (bad cholesterol) and increases HDL (good cholesterol).

- **Heart Rate** The number of cardiac contradictions per minute is called heart rate. If a 10-week training programme is allotted to an individual whose initial resting heart rate is 72 beats per minute, after the training, his resting heart rate may be reduced upto 10 beats per minute.

  Thus, a proper and long-term training programme decreases the resting heart rate.

- **Stroke Volume** The volume of blood pumped into the heart with every heartbeat is known as the stroke volume. In an untrained male, it is 50-70 ml/beat. In a trained male athlete, it may be 70-90 ml/beat. The stroke volume increases in response to the intensity of the exercises and also pumps more blood when required.

- **Blood Flow** Regular exercise increases blood flow in the body. During exercises, muscles need more blood, then body increases number of capillaries. The existing capillaries also open wider.

Or

Personality is basically a set of characteristics like attitude, habits, traits, etc., possessed by a person which greatly influence his motivation, emotion and behaviour in different situations. It reveals the psychological make up of an individual through his behaviour.

Personality is a dynamic and continuous process of learning in which an individual acquires different psychological characteristics. The word 'personality' is also used to represent all the factors inherited or acquired, which make up an individual.

Modern Day Types of Personality

Nowadays, the personality has four basic types. These are as follows

- **Personality Type A** These personalities are described as competitive and high achievers. They have high sense of time and always try to finish their job in time. They are always found busy. They can be easily aroused to anger, hostility and aggression.

- **Personality Type B** These personalities are extrovert in nature. They are very entertaining and not easily stressed. They express their emotions appropriately and cope with stress effectively.

  They can be achievers but still they do not want to be competitive. They can delay the work and try to do at the last moment.

- **Personality Type C** These personalities try to spend a lot of time on finding about how the things work. They are very cautious and reserved in nature. They are interested in accuracy, rationality and logic.

  They are not assertive and always suppress their own desires and emotions. They are more susceptible to depression as compared to type A and type B.

- **Personality Type D** They have a negative outlook towards life and are pessimistic. They are characterised as those people who resist any form of change and prefer the monotony of routine.

  They are not adventurous and always resist responsibility. The repetition allows them to become very skilled.

  They withdraw as a result of fear of rejection. The main cause of depression is suppressing the emotions for long periods of time.

9. Endurance is the ability to do sports movement with the desired quality and speed under the conditions of fatigue.

   According to **Harre** (1986), "Endurance is the ability to resist fatigue." It is measured by the duration of an activity or how long an exercise can be continued.

   According to the duration of the activity, the endurance is classified into following types

   - **Speed Endurance** It is the ability to resist fatigue in activities that last upto 45 seconds. For example, 400 m sprint race.

     Speed endurance is mainly dependent on the power and capacity of energy production.

- **Short-term Endurance** It is the ability to resist fatigue in activities that range from 45 seconds to 2 minutes. For example, 800 m race. This endurance depends on strength and speed endurance.

- **Medium-term Endurance** It is the ability to resist fatigue in activities that range from 2 minutes to 11 minutes. For example, 1500 m race.

  This endurance also depends on strength and speed endurance, but upto a limited degree.

- **Long-term Endurance** It is the ability to resist fatigue in activities that last more than 11 minutes. For example, marathon, that requires such type of endurance.

- **Continuous Training** This method was developed by **Dr Van Aaken**. Continuous training involves continuous running activity or exercise without rest or pause. It allows the body to work from its aerobic energy stores to improve overall fitness and endurance.

  Benefits of continuous training include fat burning, muscle building, and increasing maximum aerobic potential.

  For example, long distance running at a stretch.

Or

A sports person can increase his/her flexibility in the following ways

By Dynamic Stretching It refers to putting muscular effort along with movement of the body. For example kicking action, moving arm in circular motion.

By Active Stretching Under this, the muscles are stretched without moving the limbs such as standing on one leg for 30 seconds. This exercise increases flexibility.

By Static Passive Stretching It refer to stretching muscles without moving the limbs. But an external force is applied to hold the stretching position, for ex. bringing your leg high upto waist and then holding it there with your hand.

Ballistic Stretching It refers to stretching up to the maximum by swinging of the limbs in rhythm, like swimming of hands from side to side, upwards and backwards.

PNF Stretching It involves both stretching and contraction of specific muscle groups. this exercise needs an external help. Such as stretching the legs upwards one by one and holding of each leg by a partner for resistance. These stretching exercises can improve the flexibility of a sports person.

Practice Paper 2*
(Unsolved)

General Instructions

■ Time : **2 Hours**
■ Max. Marks : **35**

1. There are 9 questions in the question paper. All questions are compulsory.
2. Question no. 1 is a Case Based Question, which has five MCQs. Each question carries one mark.
3. Question no. 2-6 are Short Answer Type Questions. Each question carries 3 marks.
4. Question no. 7-9 are Long Answer Type Questions. Each question carries 5 marks.
5. There is no overall choice. However, internal choice have been provided in some questions.
   Students have to attempt only one of the alternatives in such questions.

** As exact Blue-print and Pattern for CBSE Term II exams is not released yet, so the pattern of this paper is designed by the author on the basis of trend of past CBSE Papers. Students are advised not to consider the pattern of this paper as official. It is just for practice purpose.*

Case Based Questions

1. Raman attended a Football Tournament. During the final match Shyam, one of the players fell down and was injured on the shoulder. He was immediately given first aid by the coach Mr. Raghav, who had the knowledge of first aid. Warm-up session is essential for players to avoid any serious injuries during the match. Example. Dislocation and fracture, Sprain and Strain. $(1 \times 5 = 5)$

   (i) Breakage of bones is called ________.

   (a) Fracture
   (b) Sprain
   (c) Contusion
   (d) Laceration

   (ii) Contusion is also known as ________.

   (a) Abrasion
   (b) Bruise
   (c) Bone
   (d) Tendons

   (iii) The first-aid given to sprain injury are

   (a) Applying muscle ointment
   (b) Following doctor advice
   (c) Giving massage to affected part
   (d) RICE

   (iv) In RICE, R stands for ________ to the injured limb.

   (a) Rest
   (b) Remember
   (c) Required
   (d) Resist

   (v) Hard tissue injuries take place in bones and ________.

   (a) Elbow
   (b) Upper arm bone
   (c) Cartilages
   (d) lower back

Short Answer Type Questions $(3 \times 5 = 15)$

2. Explain any three types of the coordinative abilities.   (3)

Or Write short notes on static active and static passive stretching.

3. What measures could be adopted to generate confidence among disable students.   (3)

4. Describe the provisions of any one asana which is used to cure diabetes.   (3)

Or Discuss the causes of back pain and suggest ways to prevent it.

5. Differentiate between strain and sprain.   (3)

6. Everyone in class thinks that Ram is extrovert. What do you mean by this sentence and enlist the characteristics of extrovert.   (3)

Or Why circuit training method is followed by large number of people?

Long Answer Type Questions $(5 \times 3 = 15)$

7. Assess the ways in which physical activities would be beneficial for Children With Special Needs (CWSN)?   (5)

Or What do you understand by disorder? Discuss any two disorder commonly found in the students.

8. Personality is multi-dimensional in nature. Elaborate.   (5)

Or Why it is important to include exercises in the daily curriculum of the schools?

9. In the context of the sports injury, discuss the R.I.C.E. therapy in detail.   (5)

Or What precautions need to be taken by students while playing, so they do not get any injury?

Answers

1.   (i) (a)   (ii) (b)   (iii) (d)   (iv) (a)   (v) (c)

Practice Paper 3* (Unsolved)

General Instructions

■ Time : **2 Hours**
■ Max. Marks : **35**

1. There are 9 questions in the question paper. All questions are compulsory.
2. Question no. 1 is a Case Based Question, which has five MCQs. Each question carries one mark.
3. Question no. 2-6 are Short Answer Type Questions. Each question carries 3 marks.
4. Question no. 7-9 are Long Answer Type Questions. Each question carries 5 marks.
5. There is no overall choice. However, internal choice have been provided in some questions.
   Students have to attempt only one of the alternatives in such questions.

*As exact Blue-print and Pattern for CBSE Term II exams is not released yet, so the pattern of this
paper is designed by the author on the basis of trend of past CBSE Papers. Students are advised
not to consider the pattern of this paper as official. It is just for practice purpose.*

Case Based Questions

1. Sadaf is a student of class VII and is suffering from the Asthma. During a recent medical check-up at school, she was adviced to practice yoga and participate in sports activities. $(1 \times 5 = 5)$

(i) The yoga instructor of the school has asked Sadaf to perform.

(a) Vakrasana   (b) Sukhasana

(c) Shavasana   (d) Urdhwa Hastasana

(ii) In asthma, suffering person faces difficulties in

(a) walking   (b) sleeping

(c) breathing   (d) eating

(iii) Which part of body is affected during asthama?

(a) Lungs   (b) Stomach

(c) Liver   (d) Intestine

(iv) _______ is done in lying posture.

(a) Chakrasana   (b) Vajrasana

(c) Parvatasana   (d) Gomukhasana

(v) _______ is the another name of gomukhasana.

(a) Wheel pose   (b) Cow face pose

(c) Mountain pose   (d) Fish pose

Short Answer Type Questions $(3 \times 5 = 15)$

2. Discuss any two sports injuries in brief. (3)

Or What measure can be followed to prevent sport injuries like laceration?

3. Explain Rhythm and Adaptation ability. (3)

4. Write a short note on either emotional dimension or social dimension of personality. (3)

Or Describe any two components/parts of the Big Five Theory.

5. Shed light on the salient features of the asanas. (3)

Or "Poverty may lead to disability in an individual." Elaborate.

6. What do you mean by PRICE Therapy? Write a short note on it. (3)

Or "Aggression of a sports person causes harm to him." Examine.

Long Answer Type Questions $(5 \times 3 = 15)$

7. Differentiate between dynamic and static strength. Also, discuss any one method of improving strength. (5)

Or Describe training method of any one of the following in detail - (a) Speed (b) Flexibility.

8. If anyone is regularly practicing exercises then what effect can be seen over the muscular system of a body. (5)

Or Ram is known for his high endurance capacity. His endurance is mainly determined by which factors?

9. What do you mean by disability etiquettes in general? What would be consequences if these etiquettes are not followed? (5)

Or Discuss the benefits and contraindication of any two yogas of your choice.

Answers

1.   *(i) (b)*   *(ii) (c)*   *(iii) (a)*   *(iv) (a)*   *(v) (b)*

9 789325 797024

Printed by Libri Plureos GmbH in Hamburg, Germany